Love vs. Sin
in Catholicism

Catherine D. Seawell

The Catholic Church is one of the oldest and most widespread religious organizations in the world. Most people are familiar with the Church in some way, but very few know what it is like to be a sexual or gender minority while being raised in a religion as conservative and set in its ways as the Catholic Church. We know that queer people do not stop existing just because they are religious, but not much is known about the sense-making that goes into performing both queer and Catholic identities. Narratives are particularly important tools of both sense-making and performance for individuals, and so these narratives were examined to better understand their experiences.

Through interviews and surveys, I listened to queer former Catholics tell their stories and then examined how these participants made sense of their experiences with the Catholic Church as a sexual/gender minority. Results showed a variety of ways the Church teaches and enforces the gender binary and [hetero]sexuality, along with a variety of core, shared experiences for queer former Catholics. Participants' narratives revealed how difficult the queer Catholic identity can be to hold, the inherent burden that comes from being queer, and four thematic stages of ideological integration/deconstruction. These results indicate a lack of support for minority members in the Catholic Church of America, an inherent ideological difference between Hispanic Catholicism and American Catholicism, and a greater need for spaces for queer folks who were raised Catholic to have spaces to share these stories and to find others with similar backgrounds.

KEYWORDS: Catholic; identity; narratives; queer; trauma; identity work

ACKNOWLEDGMENTS

First and foremost, I am so incredibly grateful to the individuals who were willing to share their stories with me. Thank you for allowing me a glimpse into your personal experiences as queer people raised Catholic, and for doing so with such honesty and insight. I thoroughly appreciate everything you shared— laughs, tears, verbiage, and everything in between— and I cannot thank you enough for your time. In that same vein, a huge thank you for everyone who helped connect participants and me. Without you all, this research would not have reached completion.

I would next like to thank my committee for their endless support, especially on short notice and with tight deadlines. Dr. Lindsey Thomas, I would not be the scholar or person I am today if it weren't for your support, both in this endeavor and my journey through academia thus far. Thank you for always asking how I was doing in a way that conveyed how genuinely you cared, and for bringing that same genuine compassion into your mentorship. Dr. John Baldwin, thank you for sharing your seemingly endless intelligence with me through this undertaking and the many others you have mentored me through. Your passion for learning and your collection of bad jokes have never failed to inspire and bring a much-needed smile to some of the most stressful times of my life so far. Dr. Andrew Ventimiglia, thank you for agreeing to be on this committee upon first meeting me, even when I was not entirely sure where exactly we were going with this. Your excitement for this research, belief in me, and continued encouragement through the process have been instrumental pushing me to make this the best paper it can be. You three are some of the most intelligent, kind, and genuine humans I have ever gotten the chance to work with, and I am grateful for your influence. I am a better writer, researcher, teacher, and human because of you all.

To my family, without whom I literally could not physically be here, I am also grateful. Dad, thank you for biting your tongue when I told you my thesis topic, for lending me your copy of the Catechism, and for continuing to cheer me on even if you didn't agree with the subject I'm writing on. Mom, thank you for all the texts and calls, especially the ones when I was in tears or about to scream in frustration. I know that having you two as parents helped shape me into the quirky, stubborn, sometimes argumentative, but always compassionate person I am today; your support as I forge my own paths forward means the world. To my siblings and my nephew, I love you with all my heart, and hearing your voices and seeing your pictures really have been bright spots in some bleak places.

To the ones I was lucky to call both friends and colleagues, thank you. Madison Wilson, I could not have asked for a better research partner to start grad school with. I love the research we have done, and I cannot wait to continue writing and publishing with you as we grow as scholars. (Here's to tackling publication after we get these degrees checked off!) Ertemisa Godinez, from coffee dates and providing sweets to circus nights and moral support, you are one of the best friends and colleagues I have ever had, and I am grateful for your insight on all things. Elizabeth Reed, from crystals to plants to honesty when I need it, thanks for being a friend along this rollercoaster that we called grad school. To all my cohort colleagues at ISU, I am grateful for the opportunities to learn with you and cannot wait to see where you all go in the future.

To the friends and lovers who also supported me through this program, thank you for keeping me on Earth when I thought my head was going to explode. Jill Sackville, thank you for being a friend for life, my person I can pick right back up with no matter how long ago we left off; I love you. Ashton Bauer, from my random roommate freshman year to the dancing queen whose arm carries the twin to my firefly tattoo, your constant belief in me and moral support through mundane tasks have literally gotten me through more assignments in my academic career than I can count; I love you. Victoria Mann, whose love and support for me has been unmatched, I have never met anyone whose brain works the same way mine does, until I met you. I am grateful to have you in my corner; I love you. Alex Baccheschi, thank you for everything, love. We may not have taken the path we thought, but without you I still would not have gotten this far. To Daniel Edwards, who only came into my life recently, but has been nothing but a bright spot, thank you for not asking about my thesis when I asked you not to but also letting me ramble about it for what I'm sure has been dozens of hours at this point; I appreciate you, and the cat snaps, immensely.

And to every single other person who has shown me support or given me a reason to get back to work [including the upstairs neighbors who have twice stopped a breakdown because of their noisy shenanigans literally shaking the door/fan], thank you. In the same way it takes a village to raise a child, I feel wholeheartedly that this thesis—my baby—is a product of all the interactions that got me here and lead me to the information I now have.

Finally, I would like to note that while I, personally, do not harbor any warm feelings for the Catholic Church in America, I did not conduct this study with ill intent. Rather, this overlap of identities- queer and Catholic- is severely lacking academic literature coverage. Further, I am in a unique position to understand and analyze these experiences, and at the end of the day I want to support those who have had similar struggles in their lives.

T.K.N.

CONTENTS

	Page
ACKNOWLEDGMENTS	i
TABLES	vii
CHAPTER I: AN INTRODUCTION	1
CHAPTER II: REVIEW OF LITERATURE	6
Religion	6
The Catholic Church	9
Church norms & Traditions.	10
Degrees of Doctrine (by diocese, by parish).	12
Gender: A Construct Not To Be Conflated With Sex	14
Embodying Spectral Gender: Queer &Gender-Nonconforming Folks	16
Gender & sexuality as sites of potential Catholic trauma.	19
Trauma	20
Religious Trauma	21
Queer Trauma	23
Queer People's Catholic Trauma	24
Personal Narratives	25
Narrative Performance Theory as a Framework	26
The Present Study	28
CHAPTER III: METHODOLOGY	29
Research Participants	29
Eligibility Criteria	29

Recruitment	29
Participant Information	30
Data Collection	30
Eligibility Confirmation & Demographic Survey	30
Narrative Interviews	32
Data Analysis	34
Interview Transcriptions & Data Management	34
Thematic Analysis	34
CHAPTER IV: FINDINGS	36
American Catholic Teachings & Enforcements of Gender & Sexuality	36
Teachings	36
There's a rule for that role.	37
Queerness as a problem or affliction.	38
Expected integration.	40
Enforcements	41
Subtle enforcement.	41
Lack of control.	41
Lack of support.	42
Explicit enforcement.	43
Punishment.	44
Positive reinforcement.	45
Who decides what is inappropriate?	46
Tactics for Both Teaching & Enforcement	48

Traditions & Sacraments.	48
Less than loving encounters, from exclusion and ignorance to oppression and abuse.	50
Impacts of American Catholic Teachings on Participant Identity Performances	52
To Be Queer & Catholic	53
The Burden of Queerness	55
Four Thematic Stages of Queer-Religious Identity Reconciliation	56
Control & submission.	57
"This ain't it."	57
"Recovering Catholic": Ideological integration and/or deconstruction.	60
Choosing self: In which identity is more fully realized & embraced.	63
Exceptions	64
Summary	66
CHAPTER V: DISCUSSION	67
Summary of Results & Research Considerations	67
Contributions to Queer & Religious Identity Literature	69
Theoretical Implications	70
Practical Implications	73
Study Limitations	74
Directions for Future Research	75
Conclusion	77

TABLES

Table	Page
1. Participant Information	31

CHAPTER I: AN INTRODUCTION

"Love the sinner, hate the sin," is a common phrase uttered among many Catholics and some other groups of Christians regarding homosexuality and other identities that are considered contradictory to their view of their God's plan. It is surprising that a community that is rooted in sharing the love of Jesus emphasizes loving sinners but hating their sins, especially when we look at how that mindset translates to queer people. Jesus said love everybody, but in loving queer people, Catholics (and other demographics of Christians) twisted Jesus's words to mean loving them *despite* or apart from their queerness. This attitude, in itself, is queerphobic, as queer people not only tend to consider themselves inseparable from their queerness but also find empowerment through embracing their gender and sexual identities. Therefore, this mentality can be damaging to queer individuals, despite the supposedly positive intent of phrases like "love the sinner, hate the sin" in reference to homosexuality or other forms of queerness. Further, the "love the sinner" part of the phrase rings hollow because people do not ignore, harass, attempt to change, or otherwise discriminate against people they actually love. These dynamics are important given their role in the formation of queer Catholic identities, yet, literature on the overlap of queer and Catholic identities, or even on how religious actors seek to separate gender and sexual identity from individuals, is hard to come by.

Before I further elaborate on this paradoxical standpoint, I first must draw on Butler's (2001) argument for giving an account of oneself as a researcher and reflect on my own identities and perspectives for transparency, as I am a member of the demographic group being studied (queer former Catholics). I recognize fully that not every queer person who has ever been Catholic has trauma from their experiences, but I would like to use this study to give voice to those who, like me, do have trauma from their Catholic upbringing. To avoid the assumption that all people have experiences like mine, I first would like to disclose my own experiences. In doing so I can provide my background on why I am conducting this study and disclose any potential biases I may bring with me.

I have extensive experience as a queer person in and around the Catholic Church in the United States. I have experienced firsthand the harm of the perspectives on gender the Church and its organizations perpetuate, despite the lack of literature on the harm of these perspectives. My family was Protestant Christian, first Lutheran then Presbyterian. When I was very young, my father did not really attend church with my mom and me (my mom calls this his "young agnostic phase"). After a couple of years of this that included a falling out between my mother and the church pastor, my sister was born, and my dad took us all to the Presbyterian church in town that his family attended. This was the church I remember growing up in the most, from preschool into elementary school and later the beginning of middle school. All was then rather stable in our Presbyterian love-and-light church community and our household until my parents went on a Catholic retreat called "Cursillo" the summer after I finished fourth grade.

Long story short, they each had a life-changing experience thanks to the love they experienced there. At the same time, the organization that ran the Presbyterian church my family attended declared that homosexuals would be allowed to be pastors and run churches. Both my parents had problems with this, and both referenced the Bible to support their claims. On top of that backing, my mother also carries with her the traumas of her first "adult" relationship that became cyclically toxic and ended for the last time with her boyfriend breaking up with her by coming out as gay and blaming her for it. For this reason, any time anything noticeably not-straight, also known as queer, came up in any situation, my mom's automatic response was an eye roll and a disgusted "ugh" like she was gagging or going to vomit.

Because of this and a multitude of other reasons, my dad started researching the beliefs of other Christian denominations that aligned more with how he viewed/understood the biblical answers to today's questions. During the summer between my fifth and sixth-grade years, my parents were (unbeknownst to me at the time) spending hours each night arguing about theology and what direction was right for our family. My dad "felt called to the Catholic Church" for a variety of reasons, while my mom was more hesitant. By the end of that summer, however, my parents had come to an agreement to join the Church as a family. They had no idea that the challenges of converting to Catholicism were only just beginning, and I was the next person they had to convince.

I was twelve years old, and I spent summer nights sitting across from my dad at various tables having theological debates, each of us with our personal Bibles open in front of us. We quoted passages back and forth and discussed their implications at length. Eventually, he won me over, and I accepted our family's joining the Church. I wound up being confirmed two years earlier than most kids, as a sixth grader, which meant the Church then viewed me as an adult, despite my being only 13. Indeed, I was treated like an adult long before I stopped being a child, by both my parents and the church. At this point, I was fully committed to my identity as a devout Catholic and had already begun following my parents' examples, slinging that phrase, "love the sinner, hate the sin," with surprising regularity.

It was not until late junior high or early high school that I really started to meet queer people of any kind, and it took me until I was sixteen to begin to understand that being gay – or in any way queer – is not a choice. Up until that point, and honestly even for a bit after, I continued parroting the phrase, "love the sinner, hate the sin," at my friends who were struggling with their sexualities, oblivious to how damaging that was to them as people and to our relationships. Not only did people not choose to be gay, but they also did not deserve the ridicule that my family, my church community, and even I gave them.

After coming to understand sexuality as not a choice, I started experiencing what I now know was internalized homophobia. For example, I remember being sixteen or seventeen and having a nightmare that one of my future children would be gay, and then I would be forced to choose between my religious family and my child. Without a doubt, I knew I would choose my child. I rationalized that it was one thing if I were gay and hiding it, but I would never expect anyone else to not be fully themselves. Plus, I was straight anyway, so it was not like I was hiding anything. Right?

Looking back at that memory is both sad and so funny to me. It is heartbreaking that my biggest fears were due to my religious upbringing. It is even sadder that when I look back, I can recognize that as the first time I began to choose between my inner child and my family's wishes. However, as a pansexual twenty-something, I laugh thinking back to those times of my life when I was so adamant to everyone – especially myself – that I was straight.

Now I identify as genderfluid, which usually gets simplified down to nonbinary when I do not feel like taking the time or energy to explain how gender is fluid to whomever I am talking to. I use she and they pronouns, as in I am perfectly comfortable with "she," but I feel so loved and seen when people call me "they." I came out as bisexual to my inner circle during my sophomore year of college, and then during my senior year of college, I officially started identifying as pansexual. I did not start identifying as genderfluid until closer to starting graduate school, as these things take time and self-acceptance that I did not have before leaving my parents' home and the Catholic Church.

Because of these varied but impactful experiences in my own life, I am driven to explore how, if at all, other individuals might have been impacted by experiences related to religion, specifically Catholicism, and queer identity. To this end, I reviewed literature surrounding religion, specifically the Catholic Church; gender, sex, and sexuality; the experiences of queer and gender-nonconforming people; the intersectional traumas that come from being a gender or sexual minority and being in such a conservative religion to form a strong research foundation; and, finally, some background on the narrative paradigm and how it applies to the study at hand. From there, I conducted interviews with other queer or otherwise gender-nonconforming individuals who had significant formational experiences with the Catholic Church. The specifics of the interviews covered formative experiences growing up in and around the Church that shaped the way they made sense of gender, gender roles, sex, sexuality, religion, and the traumas that occurred in these spaces. The rest of this thesis will review these findings and their implications.

CHAPTER II: REVIEW OF LITRATURE

To adequately and academically explore the traumas that queer former Catholics have incurred, religion, Catholicism, trauma, queerness, and their culmination all must be unpacked. In order to best understand the layers of intersectional interaction at work in queer former Catholics' narratives, let us start with the more basic conceptualizations in this study before building to their interactions. To understand the purpose of this study, one must first have a basic understanding of my approach to religion.

Religion

I approach organized religion through the lens of social constructionism and social interactionism, as this perspective lends itself to the explanation of how different frameworks for viewing and interpreting the world not only reflect but constitute reality (Berger & Luckmann, 1967; Blumer, 1969; Orsi, 2010). These different frameworks create social institutions, such as religions, which provide frameworks of interpretation for interacting with the world around us (Berger & Luckmann, 1967). Berger and Luckmann (1967) define religion as socially constructed realities in which people ascribe spiritual values and social order. Further, in the institutionalization of religion, there is a certain amount of implied historicism and control, or in other words every religion is a product of its history and has some degree of control over its followers (Berger & Luckmann, 1967), which will be touched on again in the Religious Trauma section.

The prevalence of religiosity is not an exact calculation, but the majority of Americans are raised in families with some kind of religious belief (Etengoff & Daiute, 2015). Indeed, according to Pew Research Center, nearly three-quarters of the United States population is at least somewhat religious (Pew, 2020). Religious involvement is often thought of as positive and having healing influences on some lives (Bergin, 1991; Dein, 2020). Some previous research supports a correlation between religious involvement and better psychological well-being, with higher levels of religious involvement tending to correlate with lower levels of depression, fewer suicidal thoughts/attempts, and less abuse of drugs and alcohol (Dein, 2020; Dein et al., 2012; Moreira-Almeida et al., 2006). While religiosity does not seem to improve one's likelihood to experience trauma, an individual's religiosity does impact, and often improves, perceptions of traumatic events (Pecchioni et al., 2011). In addition to these benefits, for those individuals with higher-stress living conditions, such as the elderly and those with disabilities or illnesses, there is an even stronger correlation between church attendance and mental fortitude (Moreira-Almeida et al., 2006).

Researchers have found that belonging to a religion, including Catholicism, has many benefits, from increased psychological well-being to lower levels of drug abuse (Dein et al., 2012). However, religions, like any other organization, have both light and dark sides (Baum, 2011; Harris et al., 2008). Those dark sides can be seen in many ways, sometimes in the form of legitimizing regimes that are otherwise deemed unjust, other times creating contempt between religious individuals and those outside their religion (Baum, 2011). Specifically, the benefits for many members of a religion do not outweigh the harm for minorities. Not everyone who is a minority in their religion has my trauma, but many gender and sexual minority (GSM) individuals do have trauma from this, and those traumas deserve to be explored academically.

The same religious frameworks that especially benefit these compromised populations can also bring harm to queer individuals (Harris et al., 2008; Moreira-Almeida et al., 2006). In the cases of queer people, higher levels of independently made religious decisions, as opposed to deferring to other religious authorities, have been found to predict lower levels of internalized homophobia, higher levels of sexual identity development, and fewer internal conflicts (Harris et al., 2008). In other words, queer people who make religious decisions based on how they feel rather than what a religious authority says have better mental health and fewer internal struggles than their counterparts who defer to religious authority before their own instincts or thoughts, especially when that religious authority is particularly conservative. Although little research to date has focused on the demographic and denominational differences between various religious affiliations and spiritual practices, further research in this area could lend greater insights into specifics of experiences and the differentiation between positive and negative religious behaviors (Johnston, 2021). In the words of Saroglou et al. (2020), "These findings suggest a somewhat conservative, moralistic view of religion" (p. 570); in other words, this notion of the social construction of reality confirms the idea that religious morality is normative as opposed to a prosocial consequence of personal beliefs. In a country where church and state are supposed to be separate, viewing conservative religious ideas as normative can pose a danger for the people whose beliefs do not align with the religious ideologies.

There is a related, potentially intertwined, moralizing tradition of religious influence in America that generally leans Conservative and can be traced back to the Puritanical roots of the United States (Steensland et al., 2000; Uhlmann et al., 2011). Americans exhibit more conservative, often religiously influenced, ideologies than most other developed nations of the world, especially about personal and sexual identity performances (Sanchez-Burks, 2004; Uhlmann et al., 2011). Though not every American religious organization is as conservative as the original Puritanical and Catholic settlements, Americans who do participate in these more traditional religions tend to lean more conservatively than members of the same religions elsewhere in the world.

The Catholic Church

Catholicism is one particular denomination of Christianity, among the variety of religious ideologies in the United States, and it is a historically widespread framework. Catholics trace their faith back to the Roman crucifixion of Christ, just as Catholic bishops can trace their lineage of vows back to St. Paul (Catholic Church, 1997; Pauly, 2018). According to the *Catechism of the Catholic Church*, otherwise referred to as "the Catechism," the Catholic Church itself can be defined as "the Church established by Christ on the foundation of the Apostles, possessing the fullness of the means of salvation which he has willed: correct and complete confession of faith, full sacramental life, and ordained ministry in apostolic succession" (Catholic Church, 1997, p. 870). Bearing this definition in mind, Catholicism can more generally be understood as the beliefs and practices associated with the Catholic Church, which believers interpret to have been established by Christ (Pauly, 2018). While most religious organizations operate differently from one another, the Catholic Church is not beholden to its stakeholders the way that most institutions, even religious ones, are beholden to stakeholders and board members (Fortunato, 2021).

The Catholic Church was formed over 2,000 years with the aim of converting the whole world to Christianity, and that goal has been evident in many Church-sanctioned actions throughout history (Baum, 2011; Pauly, 2018; Serini, 2019). However, in 1965, the Vatican startled the world and announced its newfound respect for other world religions, partially changing many theological positions Catholics had taken historically (Baum, 2011). To this day, many conservative Catholics remain ignorant, perhaps by choice, of the Church's change of heart on this matter decades ago, often in favor of local church leaders' teachings, which is just one of many examples of how Catholic ideologies are not as universal as some may believe, despite foundational beliefs being codified (Baum, 2011).

Church norms and Traditions.

In this study I consider the interactions of Catholic organizational norms and queer identities in narratives of situational threat, a step beyond the similar interplay of gender, situational threat, and organizational norms identified and discussed by Walton and Kemmelmeier (2012). This step beyond Walton and Kemmelmeier's (2012) work specifically is the additional consideration of the secular nature of the organization being studied. Every organization has organizational norms and traditions, and the Catholic Church is no exception. Faith traditions of any kind are rooted in the stories shared, such as those in religious texts (Serini, 2019). This is particularly true in Catholicism because stories of role models are found both biblically and historically, such as the lives of the saints (Serini, 2019). Catholic intellectual tradition, rooted in Jewish and Greek practices, is an ever-growing and expanding theological and philosophical skeleton of the Church that is further supported by various scholarly works (Fritz, 2017).

Traditions in the Church are maintained in a way similar to that of other institutions but also develop and expand to meet present needs in the stability that the institutional home provides (Fritz, 2017). This does not mean that the Church's traditions always accommodate their times, but it does point out that the way Catholic intellectual tradition has developed through a series of historic questions and responses that have then been adopted into new or altered traditions (Fritz, 2017). These Catholic traditions have contributed to Church norms and culture, the very culture Fortunato (2021) criticizes as being the root of a lot of the problems in the Catholic Church today. Culture itself both maintains and changes organizations, and larger organizations with more memory are often slower to change than other organizations (Weick, 2006). In this way, we can understand how the Church's 2,000-year-old culture is very slow to change or accept new roles (Serini, 2019).

This slow-to-change side of Catholic ideology starts to explain why it often does not coexist easily with more progressive ideologies. One example of this resistance to change can be seen in the identities "Catholic" and "feminist," which are seen to be at odds with one another, completely incompatible (Kalven, 2003; Pauly, 2018; Zuk & Zuk, 2020). This is both because the Church has been openly hostile towards feminist ideas and actions and also because, historically, feminists have claimed there was no room for Catholics in feminist spaces (Kalven, 2003; Pauly, 2018). Gender equality gained popularity in Protestant countries years before it did in Catholic countries, which makes sense when we consider that the Catholic Church firmly opposed the first wave of feminism in Europe (Wilcox & Jelen, 1993). Still, many people today consider themselves both Catholic and feminist (Coburn et al., 2019; Pauly, 2018), despite these stances of the Church and Catholic ideology portraying feminism to be threatening to traditional family values and social order (Zuk & Zuk, 2020).

Not only is Catholic ideology misaligned with numerous progressive ideologies, but other norms of the U.S. Catholic Church further separate most American Catholics from the rest of the world. Cover-ups of any various amounts of information from an audience are not unusual in any institution, but the Catholic Church has been particularly prone to concealing cases of interpersonal abuse, ranging from abuses of power to verbal, physical, and sexual abuse cases, a way of addressing (or not) threats to their credibility (Carey, 2020; Fortunato, 2021; Kaylor, 2008). The Church has been divided for decades between people calling for more transparency and the people who most benefit from the secrecy and lower standards of accountability (Carey,

2020). While there are many aspects of the Church that lay people do not get to view because they are not ordained and have not taken particular vows, the variance in ideological implementations in Catholic spaces, particularly when comparing diocese or parishes to one another, can be recognized by anyone who attends more than one church for mass in their life

Degrees of Doctrine (by diocese, by parish).

While there has been no significant resolution of any scale to this cultural tug-of-war, smaller branches within the Church, such as dioceses or even parishes, are easier to change ideologically, regarding cover-up beliefs (meaning the Church beliefs that it is okay to not give members all information) or nearly any other political matter in the Church, for a variety of reasons. The hierarchy and uniqueness of the organizational structure of the Catholic Church in the US cannot be understated, as they play a role in the perpetuation and handling of difficult issues such as sexual and child abuse (Maier & Christ, 2017). A critical structural complexity of Catholicism is the prioritization of subsidiarity, a principle "in which decision-making is delegated to the lowest appropriate level" (Maier & Crist, 2017, p. 168). Because of this delegation practice, Catholic dioceses enjoy immense operational freedom (Maier & Christ, 2017). The United States Conference of Catholic Bishops (USCCB), for example, claims to be "an assembly of the hierarchy of bishops who jointly exercise pastoral functions on behalf of the Christian faithful of the United States and the U.S. Virgin Islands" and "promote the common good which the Church offers humankind" (USCCB, 2022). By these identifications, which were found on their "About Us" page, the USCCB appears to be an official authority with the power to make and enforce policy (Maier & Crist, 2017; USCCB, 2022). However, the USCCB has no authority under canon law, as every Catholic bishop on the planet answers only to the current pope (Catholic Church, 1997; Maier & Crist, 2017). Because bishops, each of whom oversees a diocese, are free to interpret and enact all policies presented to them by the USCCB as they see fit, the organization is largely unfit to handle crises, as was seen in the Church's handling of clergy abuse scandals (Catholic Church, 1997; Maier & Crist, 2017). The Vatican's reluctance to hold bishops more accountable has only served to worsen their public perception, particularly after cases of clergy abuse (Maier & Crist, 2017). In other words, many American Catholics, or at least the Diocese they attend, choose to follow the more conservative USCCB as opposed to Vatican guidance.

A key factor in the success of handling crises, be it between dioceses or between parishes, is transparency between clergy and lay people, as some younger Church leaders are starting to engage in more dialogue around these issues (Carey, 2020). While church cultures are bound to differ some between parishes, the differences between cultures in various U.S. dioceses are astonishing. In the same way the Church's culture, as a whole, only seems to change, even if it is slight change, when there is a new pope. The individual dioceses can change drastically with the installment of a new bishop, as the interpreter for and leader of the diocese has a different perspective (Catholic Church, 1997; Maier & Crist, 2017; Serini, 2019). For this reason, among other geopolitics in the country, American dioceses are extensively varied in their commitments, capacities, and competencies (Fortunato, 2021; Maier & Crist, 2017).

While there are currently no promising signs that the Church as a whole or even nationwide will give a sincere attempt at holding all Church leaders more accountable for misuse of power or doctrine, despite evidence that letting crises speak is both hard and necessary, Catholic institutions have occasionally organized and worked to support trauma survivors (Carey, 2020; Fortunato, 2021; Maier & Crist, 2017). In 2002, the Voice of the Faithful emerged to speak for more accountability in the Catholic clergy, yet Catholic priests and bishops alike were quick to condemn the members of this group of heresy (Kaylor, 2008). In 2018, a focus group and task force were created to give support to students and faculty at a Catholic university after another round of sexual abuse cases involving clergy came to light, yet their efforts were halted by the COVID pandemic (Fortunato, 2021). Catholics continue to view self-satisfaction as destructive to society, and also tend not to acknowledge the harm that has been caused in the name of their religion (Zuk & Zuk, 2020). The present study is a product of the belief that adding to the body of literature supporting survivors of Catholic trauma will eventually lead to change that reduces the harm brought into the world through the Church. Further, some of this trauma is also a product of gender norms and enforcement.

Gender: A Construct not to be Conflated with Sex

Sex and gender are often conflated, especially culturally (see Duxbury, 2014), but they are not the same. Sex is the biologically (primarily visual interpretation of external physical characteristics) based binary of male and female, which is assigned at birth by doctors (Deaux, 1985; Dyer & Gunnell, 1993; Thorne et al., 2019). This assignment of newborns' sex to male and female is then transcribed into certain expectations for individuals; transmuting sex assignment into gender performance is known as sex typing, which is defined as the process of transcribing male and female into what it means to be masculine and feminine (Bem, 1981). Meanwhile, gender refers to psychological features that are associated with different biological states, and it can be assigned by an observer or the individual expressing the features (Deaux, 1985; Mazzuca et al., 2020).

Today, scholars regard gender as an identity that the individual can make sense of and share; unlike sex, gender exists on a spectrum, not a binary (Dyer & Gunnell, 1993; Monro, 2005). While both sex and gender are similarly steeped in societal context, and these concepts are undeniably deeply embedded in one another, gender is something we perform while sex is something we have based on genitalia (Mazzuca et al., 2020). Lay people, especially those of religious and/or conservative backgrounds, may not regard gender as any different than sex, but this is factually incorrect.

As a society, people tend to assume that individuals all experience biological sex and psychological gender in ways that align with one another, such as females feeling like women and males feeling like men (Dyer & Gunnell, 1993; Mazzuca et al., 2020; Schilt & Westbrook, 2009), but this is not always the case. Because identities reflect social categorization, they are not exclusively cognitive experiences but also are performed, embodied, and experienced in a variety of contexts (Fuist, 2016). The most prominent reason gender matters in our society is that people tend to use different tactics to approach others based on the perceived gender of the people they are communicating with (Schilt & Westbrook, 2009). Most people only perceive gender as a binary because that is how society as a collective has socially constructed gender (Mazzuca et al., 2020; Schilt & Westbrook, 2009). While scholars know that gender identity does not exist on a binary, most models of gender still reinforce the sex binary and very few of these models take into account the space between or outside of man or woman (Fiani & Han, 2018).

According to Blumer (1969), every human being interacts with everything and everyone around them based on the meanings they have assigned to those people, places, and objects. Those personal meanings come from each social interaction, and these meanings are sorted through and modified as the individual at hand interprets them (Blumer, 1969). Therefore, in order to change anything, one must first change the way one conceptualizes that item. By this definition, everything, including gender, is socially constructed.

It is critical to this study and any other study relating to gender identities that we do not continue to confuse and use these elements of personal identity—sex and gender—interchangeably (Webster, 2021). In order to avoid conflating, merging, or equating gender and sex, we must recognize the links between gender, sex, and sexuality for the links, not equal signs, that they are (Carr, 2005; Webster, 2021). Unfortunately, sex and gender are not the only terms of identity that get regularly conflated. The conflation of sex, gender, and even sexuality is problematic because it perpetuates the narrative that homosexual, bisexual, and other queer individuals are abnormal males and females (Veniegas & Conley, 2000, as cited by Carr, 2005).

Thankfully, just because a person conflates these terms now, this does not mean there is no hope for improvement in that person's understanding. Not only can one still change their assumptions of sex, gender, and sexuality, but they can also learn to de-gender and even potentially recognize themself outside of the binary (Szulc, 2020). This process of removing one's own assumptions about how inherent gender is can be referred to as de-gendering (Monro, 2019; Webster, 2021). As individuals undergo this process of de-gendering, or moving beyond gender, more fluidity is recognized – and more importantly, the fluid space between genders becomes a space in which all varieties of people can not only inhabit but thrive (Monro, 2019; Thorne et al., 2019).

Embodying Spectral Gender: Queer and Gender-Nonconforming Folks

Gender has been academically studied outside of the binary since the 1970s when terms began to be used to describe people who did not strictly present as a man or a woman, such as "psychological androgyny," for people who felt neither man nor woman and "two-spirit" which was rooted in Native American ideologies of a person who had two distinct gendered presentations (Bem, 1974; Thorne et al., 2019). In the 1970s and 1980s Sandra Bem explored sex-type roles (1974a), androgyny (1974b), and the societal roles of gender with gender schema theory (1981). "Genderqueer" began to appear academically in the late 1990s as an extension of the term "transgender"; this term was created to include individuals who were not transitioning from one point on the binary to another but were instead affirming their gender outside of those two points (Monro, 2005; Thorne et al., 2019). Today "non-binary," or "nonbinary," is an accepted term of gender identification and categorization outside of the binary (Bradford et al., 2018; Monro, 2019). On the other hand, often because of how entrenched the binary construction of gender is, even individuals questioning, rejecting, or moving across the bi-gendered schema still can only conceptualize their own experiences within the male-female dichotomy (Fiani & Han, 2018; Mazzuca et al., 2020). As more and more people openly identify as nonbinary, hopefully the burden of falling into a newer and less accepted gender category will diminish.

Currently in our society, most of the weight and responsibilities of accepting people with gender-nonconforming identities falls on those same individuals who are transgender or gender-nonconforming (Austin, 2016; McLemore, 2015). Having to constantly re-explain or defend one's identity is disheartening and exhausting; having one's identity misclassified or not recognized is psychologically disruptive (McLemore, 2015). However, as more organizations and groups in society become accepting and inclusive toward transgender and nonbinary individuals, the burden on the shoulders of these individuals lessens (Austin, 2016). In an ideal world, the experiences of trans and gender-nonconforming people would be talked about and normalized, so that these individuals are seen in the same light as their cisgender counterparts; this would lessen the pain and struggle currently associated with the trans or nonbinary experience (Austin, 2016). As these struggles diminish, so too will the rigid barriers between gender identities.

According to Szulc (2020), gender as we know it is coming to an end. Even without this potentially mind-boggling statement, the prevalence of gender non-conforming individuals is 11% of LGBTQ adults in the U.S., or approximately 1.2 million people (Dowd, 2022). Even as embedded in Western social culture as the gender binary is (see Richards, 2016), the meaning of gender in our society is no longer exhausted by the classical dichotomy of biological male and female (Mazzuca et al., 2020). More to Szulc's (2020) point, transgender rights, such as the right to a change in sex or to have one's gender identity recognized, along with the previously accepted discourses around transgender issues no longer provide sufficient frameworks to discuss individual gender identities and expressions. It is the so-called "gender outlaws," trans individuals who, in choosing to be publicly themselves, challenge heteronormative ideas about gender and identity in our society, who begin to pave the way for binary gender to begin to end (Nagoshi et al., 2017). Gender performances continue to point to gender as a fluid concept, and one that exists on a spectrum, as opposed to a rigid, stationary, or dictated identity.

As society moves towards accepting more variety in gender expressions and uses terms like nonbinary, other conflicts can arise. One such problem is that nonbinary is no longer a non-category, which makes it more complicated- and arguably contradictive or oxymoronic- to explain (Monro, 2005). In other words, nonbinary is both a gender category and an identity that resists categorization, which is admittedly confusing. However, conceptualizing non-binary as anything outside of the male and female poles of the gender binary leaves space for individuals to identify themselves without falling back into the male-female dichotomy (Fiani & Han, 2018; Mazzuca et al., 2020). Therefore, the recommended framework for thinking of gender in a way that non-binary identities make the most sense is gender pluralism, or "conceptualizing gender as plural, a spectrum, a field, or intersecting spectra or continua" (Monro, 2005, p. 37). This is how gender can be viewed as fluid and a spectrum in a way that benefits the individuals using these identifiers and also the people who are trying to better understand nonbinary and other nonconforming individuals.

Gender & sexuality as sites of potential Catholic trauma.

Queer and Catholic identity conflicts are similar to the aforementioned Catholic/feminist conflict, with the addition of other intersections to consider, such as the involuntary nature of one's internal sense of gender or sexual identity and the many ramifications of openly aligning with a queer identity in a Catholic space. The interconnectedness of gender identity and sexual identity in Catholic ideology, both complicates and compounds these potential conflicts and traumas. For example, the Church views homosexuality as if it were in contradiction with human nature, the natural order of things, and normalcy (Zuk & Zuk, 2020). Priests and Catholic fundamentalists alike argue that being homosexual comes from violating traditional values and norms (Zuk & Zuk, 2020), not biological conditioning or coding, though the Catechism does not explicitly state this (Catholic Church, 1997). Further, the Church explicitly views gender only as one's assigned sex at birth, which dictates one's role in the world, and also views any other conceptualization of gender as an ideology based on hedonism and Marxism that creates moral chaos in society, which means it would be immoral for them to support the notion of gender or the rights of sexual and gender minorities (Catholic Church, 1997; Zuk & Zuk, 2020).

Gender, and as an extension, heterosexuality, as rigid and defined by one's sex at birth is a less-explicitly documented norm that becomes more apparent with more time spent in Catholic settings, especially those settings where masses are held by more traditional priests. However, conservative Christians have long claimed that gender and sexual orientation diversity and Christianity are incompatible (Etengoff & Daiute, 2015). It is difficult to find academic literature specifically talking about the Catholic Church and its members' enforcement of gender norms and expectations, but Zuk and Zuk (2020) touch on the role the Church has in enforcing traditional gender and sexuality norms in the Polish cultural context, explaining that the Polish right "perceives both feminist and homosexual circles as a threat to the national identity associated with the Catholic religion and as a threat to the traditional family model and social order" (p. 571). Later, the same scholars posit that "the key role in the understanding of 'genderism' in Poland is played by the Catholic Church and the related centers that reproduce the traditionalist vision of the social order" (Zuk & Zuk, 2020, p. 574). These Catholic perceptions of feminism, homosexuality, and so-called 'genderism' as threats not only to the Church but to the traditional family and social order are universal and supported by the official position of the Church (Catholic Church, 1997; Zuk & Zuk, 2020). Church hierarchs repeatedly indicate, everywhere from local pulpits to the Vatican, that it is not just encouraged but required of Catholics to clearly express their opposition to the legalization of homosexual marriage because it is not the same as a sacramental heterosexual marriage and therefore should not be equated (Catholic Church, 1997; Zuk & Zuk, 2020). In other words, a negative aspect of Catholic ideology is the perception of non-Catholic people living lives that do not align with Catholic ideologies as a threat to both their institution and the world as a whole. This is problematic because the behaviors enacted because of Catholic ideologies result in othering in even the best-case scenario, and results in various detriments including trauma or even suicide in the worst-case scenarios.

Trauma

Trauma sometimes gets treated as a dirty word; much of the disgust with "trauma" is just a lack of understanding of the concept (Anderson, 2020; Johnston, 2021). Trauma has been notoriously difficult to define, because of how much distress occurs and how subjective the subject matter is that comes from traumatic events (Dalenberg et al., 2017), but in general traumatic events are any experiences that shatter a person's safe worldview to the point that a refuge no longer exists or seems to exist (Panchuk, 2018). Although there is much work left to do around defining trauma as a concept, some scholars have settled for a somewhat more precise definition of trauma as an experience of notable events that result in cognitive or emotional reactions to those or similar events at a later time (Cox et al., 2016; Dalenberg et al., 2017). Previous research has shown that people who have experienced more trauma generally experience higher amounts of psychological distress in stressful scenarios after the traumatic event(s) (Cox et al., 2016). This present study, however, is less interested in measuring trauma-related variables and more interested in understanding how people make sense of trauma(s).

Religious Trauma

Religious trauma can come from these framings or ideologies (Panchuk, 2018). While religion is not necessarily traumatic or inherently negative, it can be for many people (Bergin, 1991; Dein, 2020). Historically, many members of evangelical, fundamental, traditional, and other theologically conservative religious groups have subjected SGM individuals to discrimination and abuse, and unfortunately, these ideologies continue to penetrate religious communities (Killian et al., 2021). In many American cases, it is through the normalizing of conservative religious ideologies that trauma is dealt to individuals who do not conform to said religious ideologies, and often those most victimized perceive their strife to be directly from God (Panchuk, 2018; Ruth, 2005). Definitionally speaking, religious trauma has been defined as

> A traumatic experience perceived by the subject to be caused by the divine being, religious community, religious teaching, religious symbols, or religious practices that transform the individual, either epistemically or not-merely-cognitively, in such a way

that their capacity to participate in religious life is significantly diminished. (Panchuk, 2018, p. 517)

Other authors conceptualize religious trauma differently. One scholar explains that distinctly religious traumas are caused by something the individual associates with religion because an individual perceives the religion to have either supported someone who has perpetrated religious abuse toward them or failed to stop them, and the individual experiences post-traumatic stress that is triggered by religious objects or concepts (Tobin, 2016). Either way we conceptualize it, more evangelical teenagers have been shown to have higher levels of religious internalization, which is the internalizing and identification with religious values or beliefs (Ryan et al., 1993). Religious internalization can also lead to higher levels of internalized homophobia.

According to Panchuk (2018), "The observation that there can be a distinctly religious aftermath to the abuse inflicted in religious contexts is not new, although it has been slow to gain recognition, not only within philosophy of religion, but also within psychotherapy and theology" (p. 515). In other words, we have seen religious trauma and its ongoing effects for years, but only more recently have we been acknowledging it and dealing with it academically. One scholar who has discussed religious trauma, Theresa Tobin, works with spiritual violence victims and posits:

> While individuals whose spiritual selves are closely tied to a particular religious institution are less likely to be aware of the systemic spiritual violence against themselves or others, they are also most likely to internalize the spiritually violent perspective that does them long-term spiritual harm. (Tobin, 2016, p. 153)

Survivors of abuse in any religious context may react with symptoms typical of post-traumatic stress, but they also suffer in a way unique to their type of abuse (Panchuk, 2018; Ruth,

2005; Tobin, 2016). After all, thinking one caused God, or at least his earthly representatives, to be upset to the point of causing one harm is detrimental to that person's mental health (Panchuk, 2018; Ruth, 2005). Even if the victim of the religious mistreatment thinks they were treated unfairly, there are almost no options forward for a victim to seek reparations or assistance because of the secular nature of the authority in question (Panchuk, 2018). This adds an additional level of perceived helplessness to a victim who is already in distress and is one of many reasons people with religious trauma may not approach church members or clergy to attempt to deal with this trauma.

Queer Trauma

Being queer in any way comes with many challenges, including unfair treatment in housing, a variety of healthcare issues, and a much higher suicide rate than other demographics, it should not come as a surprise that many LGBTQ+ individuals have some level of queer trauma (Duxbury, 2014; Hart et al., 2019). Nonbinary individuals tend to have a lower quality of life and more mental health struggles than cisgender and binary trans individuals do; this is most likely due to high levels of minority stress and social discrimination (Monro, 2019). Being queer means rapidly learning the unwritten social rule of being LBGT: Work twice as hard as the person next to you and get half of the credit (Duxbury, 2014). This unwritten rule makes everything harder than necessary, which is why so many people from previous generations got so worried about their family members being out as gay or queer in the community (Duxbury, 2014). While times are changing, neither these older standards nor Catholic ideologies have fallen to the wayside.

Therefore, there are many traumatic experiences in the life of a person who does not meet our society's expectations of gender, sexuality, and performance. According to Dowd (2022), 11% of nonbinary individuals in the U.S. were exposed to conversion therapy in their youth,

53% of them reported being bullied often as a child, 82% of them faced childhood emotional abuse, and 55% of them reported being physically attacked or sexually assaulted since turning 18. Those numbers are just for nonbinary individuals; the numbers for LGBTQ+ individuals are higher still (The Trevor Project, 2022). Scholars have concluded from research that having one's identity misclassified or misrepresented is psychologically disruptive (McLemore, 2015). The experience of being misgendered undermines the belonging and coherence needs of the trans and/or nonbinary individual at hand and reflects then on how those individuals evaluate themselves and their integration into society (Duxbury, 2014; McLemore, 2015).

Queer People's Catholic Trauma

Although religious frameworks, such as Catholicism, can provide many folks with security/guidance/comfort, this is not always the case- especially when lived experiences are at odds with the framings provided by the church. Therefore, queer Catholics are in a unique position of overlapping traumas and conflicting identities (Killian et al., 2021). Family support is the best safeguard against negative mental and behavioral health outcomes like depression and suicide (Gibbs & Goldbach, 2015). However, when a queer person's family is Catholic, their family members' capacities for support are often greatly limited by their religious beliefs (Gibbs & Goldbach, 2015; Zuk & Zuk, 2020).

While more religious individuals tend to value family more highly than less religious individuals, these more religious families also have more difficulty accepting family members who are gay, queer, or otherwise gender-nonconforming than less religious families do (Etengoff & Daiute, 2015). Parents having religious beliefs that are at odds with their children's identities are associated with high levels of internalized homophobia and suicidal thoughts, along with higher rates of suicide attempts (Gibbs & Goldbach, 2015).

The degree to which queer individuals internalize the religious perspective they were raised with impacts both their levels of internalized homophobia and their ability to enact any kind of spirituality after experiencing these religious traumas (Tobin, 2016). Even if these queer individuals have addressed their parental concerns about their SGM identity, they often have to readdress these issues multiple times in their adulthood as their parents still struggle with their child's romantic relationships and other aspects of nonconformity (Etengoff & Daiute, 2015). This boundary instability only adds to the mistrust that queer people experience in the Church as a result of spiritual violence against them (Tobin, 2016). Clinical therapists have commented that the most healthy and effective mediational strategies outside of therapy result in either higher levels of parental support or a higher relational distance implemented between the queer individual and their parent(s) (Etengoff & Daiute, 2015). While leaving one's religion is a solution that has been shown to decrease internalized homophobia and increase individuals' levels of self-acceptance, leaving any institution that has been part of the structure of one's life can directly increase the odds of suicidal thoughts unrelated to the reason for leaving (Gibbs & Goldbach, 2015). The intersectionality of queer identity and religious background does not have an extensive body of literature (Killian et al., 2021), and so this study aims to add to that body of literature.

Personal Narratives

Narratives are how we make sense of and navigate everything around us- our experiences, our culture, and even our identities (Bamberg & Georgakopoulou, 2008; Richardson, 2000). No matter how small or seemingly insignificant, personal narratives are both culturally embedded and sites of notable identity work that can be seen and utilized anywhere people get together (Bamberg & Georgakopoulou, 2008; Langellier, 1999). While some scholars prefer to study master or life narratives (see Carr, 2005), examining these "big" life stories does not always answer our questions about day-to-day experiences and interactions in the ways that examining smaller, more embedded stories enables (see Bradford et al., 2018).

Further, narrative studies are growing ever more critical (Kraus, 2006; Richardson, 2000), using personal narratives to examine the impacts of power structures in society. Narratives have been regarded as the best way to explore connections between perceptions and gender or sexuality (Bradford et al., 2018; Carr, 2005; Thorne et al., 2019), and even potentially as the most useful for including contextual information in analysis, including what developmental stage a person is in, both when the story took place and at the time they tell their story (Hammack & Cohler, 2009). Therefore, in this study, I will be expanding on current findings in order to explore religious experiences alongside gender and sexuality with the most regard for the contexts in which individuals find themselves.

Narrative Performance Theory as a Framework

The narratives of Church hierarchs are spread through various media, including political debates, far-right demonstrations, and opinion videos on YouTube (Zuk & Zuk, 2020). These are just a few examples of narratives as performances, which constitute a pillar of Langellier and Peterson's (2017) Narrative Performance Theory. The other pillars of NPT include consideration for communication contexts, including the deeply embedded cultural assumptions; analysis of the rules of power and knowledge that our discourses operate within; and critical exploration of the relations of power, for example in families (Langellier & Peterson, 2017). NPT is used to characterize and explain how people make and perform, or do, their identities. The theory was originally created for family scholarship, but this study and others expand NPT to a variety of other communicative spaces.

The NPT goal this study will most utilize is the serious consideration given to the context of communication, otherwise framed as the situatedness of storytelling in relational history and cultures (Langellier & Peterson, 2017). Considerations from this goal include examining how particular meanings, materials, and social contexts are embodied or assumed (Langellier & Peterson, 2017). In other words, narratives will be analyzed with regard for context, or the entire story being told, as opposed to singular aspects.

The second goal of NPT is to analyze the impact of rules and knowledge on discourse operation, or the ways power and information influence the ways people have conversations and perform roles (Langellier & Peterson, 2017). This first research question reflects this goal, but the focus of this study is less on how power and knowledge influence the narrative performances, and more on how individuals with seemingly contradictory identities make sense of and perform those identities. Discourse is not being examined in this study, though most NPT studies do involve some level of discursive analysis.

The third goal of NPT is to critically focus on power relations, which this study aims to touch on as a secondary goal to understanding participant experiences. Hopefully through the findings of the present study, power imbalances in American Catholicism can be recognized. Overlapping power structures occur in not only Catholic churches, but also Catholic schools and Catholic households.

Logically, in the same way familial storytelling is accepted as a product of interactions in families and as a way of making sense of familial experiences, identity work occurs through narrative performance (Langellier & Peterson, 2017). That is, the stories told about an individual- and about people and characters with whom the individual identifies- alongside the stories that the individual tells about themselves, to others or themselves, are products of their interactions and sites of sense-making around their own identity or overlapping identities (Langellier & Peterson, 2017). Therefore, the study at hand will utilize Narrative Performance Theory as a framework for understanding and examining participant experiences.

The Present Study

Through this review of religious, gender, and trauma literature, questions arose around the identity performance considerations of queer people raised Catholic. To best contribute to the body of academic literature the experiences of queer folks raised in the Catholic church, I have two research questions to answer in this study. First, to understand how Church teachings are perceived by these people, I ask:

RQ1: Based on their narratives, how do queer people perceive the Catholic Church to teach and/or enforce gender and sexuality?

Second, to better understand how queer former Catholics feel they have been impacted by their upbringing, I ask:

RQ2: How do queer former Catholics describe the impact of their upbringing on their identity performance?

The following chapter will explain the methodology used for the present study.

CHAPTER III: METHODOLOGY

Research Participants

Eligibility Criteria

Participants had to meet the following criteria to be eligible to participate in the study: (a) be above the age of 18 years old, (b) currently live in the United States, (c) have had formative experiences with the Catholic Church (such as being confirmed, having regular mass attendance, or having attended a Catholic school, etc.), and (d) identify as queer in some way (in other words is a SGM member).

Recruitment

This study was submitted to and approved by the Illinois State University Institutional Review Board before recruitment began. Several recruiting strategies were implemented in hopes of a demographically broad sample. To improve chances of engaging in timely interviews, I began recruitment within their university and the surrounding community. First, community members who had previously expressed interest in studies of this nature were contacted and invited to participate. Then an invite was shared among peers to be shared through the university. Snowball sampling was also utilized, as one participant was able to recruit another person with a different perspective yet the same qualifications. Finally, a Twitter post was created to invite queer current and former Catholics to participate. Twitter was used as opposed to Facebook because Twitter is a platform where individuals are less likely to interact with their families or people who are not queer-friendly, and I did not want to put anyone eligible for this study at risk by forcing them out of the closet on social media. I sought out seven to fifteen participants but stopped seeking further participation after eight interviews because redundancy, or a lack of new codes/themes, was occurring (Guba & Lincoln, 1982). Peer debriefing was utilized frequently in the organization of codes into themes, and again during the defining of themes, to verify my perspective was accurate and as unbiased as possible, as per Guba and Lincoln's (1982) recommendation.

Participant Information

The eight participants all were in the continental United States during their interviews, and all confirmed that they met all forementioned eligibility criteria. Participant ages ranged from 19 to 26. Six participants were assigned female at birth, while two were assigned male at birth; three participants identified as women, one as a man, two as nonbinary, one as "neither a woman nor nonbinary, but femme," and one as both woman and nonbinary. Two participants identified as homosexual, five identified as bisexual, and one identified as a "lesbian-leaning bisexual." Further, one participant identified as asexual ("so technically bi-romantic and asexual"), and two participants identified as polyamorous. Participants had all left the Catholic Church before the time of their interview, with their ages of exit ranging from 13-21. Four participants currently are not religious or spiritual, while the other four have found some kind of spiritual practice outside of organized religions since their exit from the Church. Interestingly among participants, one was raised by a third order Carmelite mother, and another participant's father was a deacon when she was a child and has become a priest since her exit from the Church. For a summary of characteristics of the participants, see Table 1.

Data Collection

Eligibility Confirmation & Demographic Information Survey

Before completing an interview, all potential interviewees filled out a brief demographic survey (see Appendix A). The survey began with the list of the four eligibility requirements and asked participants to confirm that they met the eligibility requirements. Then nine demographic

Table 1

Participant Information

Pseudonym	Age	Assigned Sex at Birth	Gender Identity	Sexuality	Race	Ethnicity	Currently Religious/ Spiritual?	If yes, how?	Age 1st Queer Inkling	Age Left Church	Age 1st Came Out
Indigo	26	AFAB	Woman	Bisexual, Polyamorous	White	Latina	Yes	Spiritual/ Pagan	10	14	20
Emily	26	AFAB	Woman	Bisexual	White	n/a	No	n/a	13	19	25
Sky	25	AFAB	Nonbinary	Lesbian-leaning Bisexual	Hispanic	Latina	No	n/a	5	21	15
Juniper	25	AMAB	Nonbinary	Lesbian	White	n/a	Yes	Spiritual agnosticism	4	17	17
Adam	19	AMAB	Man	Asexual, Bisexual	White	n/a	No	n/a	14	15	16
Claire	24	AFAB	Femme Non-Woman	Bisexual	Hispanic	Latina	Yes	Brujaria	5	13	15
Hannah	23	AFAB	Woman	Homosexual	White	n/a	No	n/a	10	17	18
Aubrey	24	AFAB	Woman & Nonbinary	Bisexual, Polyamorous	White	n/a	Yes	Recovering Catholic	15	12	18

questions followed, one of which is a two-part question about current religious affiliation. Other questions included age, gender identity, sexuality, and race.

Narrative Interviews

Recall that narrative scholarship is gaining respect and traction. Langellier (1989) said that sharing narratives are how we can make sense of both our own experiences and others, and that comparison of narratives can provide valuable information to individuals and researcher alike. In 1999, Langellier posited personal narratives sit at the crux of conflicts between culture, experience, and identity. Then Kraus (2006) utilized narratives to understand how people made sense of identity and belonging. All of these aspects of the usefulness of narratives led me to conduct narrative interviews to best answer my research questions.

Personal narrative interviews were conducted over Zoom using a semi-structured interview protocol (see Appendix B) as a guide in order to reveal meanings constructed within narrative performances. While traditional social scientific interviews ask participants a set of predetermined questions, narrative interviews are set apart from other types of interviewing with the unstructured format, in which whole stories are told to the interviewer as opposed to fragments given to answer specific questions (Lindlof & Taylor, 2010). According to Riessman (2008), narrative interviewing expands on traditional interviewing because it privileges the "opening up" of topics by two active conversationalists. While participant turns may take longer than interviewer turns because they are telling "their story," there is still a conversation produced in the interactions between parties that is considered part of the narrative interview (Riessman, 2008).

To further build on this co-creation through narrative, personal narratives, and life stories in particular, are especially useful in the present study. Cohler and Hostetler (2003) explain the "life story method" as an autobiographic account of one's life through their present age, which changes as the individual ages and ascribes new meaning to their experiences. Further, life narratives serve to share not only the experiences of individuals in the contexts of their lives, but also the social contexts and even the cultural aspects that their experiences are just as rooted in (Cohler & Hosteter, 2003; Hammock & Cohler, 2009). Gender, sexuality, and religion all have their own multitudes of cultural expressions and therefore cultural impacts, which intersect and effect individuals differently (Hammock & Cohler, 2009; Tobin, 2016). Therefore, I conducted narrative interviews in conversation with participants to gain insight into the experiences of queer people with formative experiences in the Catholic Church and the impacts they felt these Catholic experiences had on them.

All interviews began with a brief introduction to the topic before asking the participants to share their life story through Catholicism and queerness, as Riessman (2008) suggests. This was done to invite the interviewee to give an honest, extended response. However, as not every respondent is comfortable sharing a prolonged account (Riessman, 2008), I also prepared and utilized an interview guide following McAdams' (2006) methodology to expand upon participants' initial life narrations as needed. Along with this semi-structured interview guide, I employed floating prompts as McCracken (1998) directs.

After participants shared their story, and, as we engaged in the life story interview, I guided the conversation to follow-up questions, either resulting from the narratives shared or still-unanswered questions. Finally, the interviewer asked more quantifiable or easily described questions, such as the age participants were introduced to Catholicism, the age they began to expect their own queerness, spiritual belief and sexuality reconciliation, and advice they might provide for queer youths in the Catholic Church today. Once participants received a final opportunity to share anything else they felt compelled to share about their experiences, they were thanked for their time and encouraged to reach out with any questions or concerns. Interviews lasted from 45 to 140 minutes each, averaging 83 minutes in length.

Data Analysis

Interview Transcription & Data Management

Interviews were recorded on my computer, either with the recording function or through Zoom, depending on the location of the participants. Each audio recording was then run through Otter, a digital transcription service that utilizes artificial intelligence, for an initial transcription before being corrected by hand to match the interview verbatim. This was practical because, in correcting and transcribing these interviews, I was also familiarizing myself with the data, which is the first step of thematic analysis (Braun & Clark, 2006). Therefore, transcription marked the start of my data analysis.

During the transcription process, protecting my participants' confidentiality was also on my mind. Names of individuals, be they participants or otherwise, were replaced with pseudonyms, and other identifying information, such as dates or locations, were either replaced in or deleted from the transcripts. All audio and transcript files were stored on a password-protected device, and audio files were deleted permanently after accurate transcripts were completed.

Thematic Analysis

Two separate thematic analyses (Braun & Clarke, 2006) of transcripts were conducted, in order to answer both research questions. Step two of the thematic analysis was to code for utterances and utilized the priming phrase "gender and (Catholic) ideas, teachings, or regulations" to know when to create codes for my first RQ (Braun & Clark, 2006). For RQ2, I repeated the process with the heuristic question, "How does the Catholic ideology impact participants?" Similar codes for each RQ were then grouped to start forming potential themes, as per step three of Braun and Clarke's (2006) approach to thematic analysis. Once themes were made exclusive, these overarching themes were named, and exemplars were chosen to represent each theme.

CHAPTER IV: FINDINGS

The current chapter presents the findings of the thematic analyses described in Chapter III, thus answering the two research questions posed in Chapter II: "Based on their narratives, how do queer people perceive the Catholic Church to teach and/or enforce gender?" and "How do queer former Catholics describe the impact of their upbringing on their identity performance?" The chapter is divided by research question, with a third section for exceptions to the overarching narrative of Catholic trauma in churches and individuals.

American Catholic Teachings and Enforcements of Gender and Sexuality

Gender and sexuality norms are taught and enforced by the Catholic Church in a variety of ways, according to participants. Once all codes were taken from the interviews, tactics for teaching were separated from tactics of enforcement, and a third category, "taught and enforced" emerged as some of the implemented tactics worked to do both.

Teachings

I labeled first theme that emerged under Church Teachings, "There's a Rule for that Role," because it encompassed both the strict gender binary and sexuality rules the Church teaches and also the Catholic belief in predetermined roles. Participant narratives of Church teachings all corroborated the Catechism teachings discussed in Chapter II, in that gender is the same as sex and the only options are man or woman. This was further supported by the theme, "Queerness as a Problem or Affliction," as all participants made mention of many Catholics' views on queerness as problematic or something one had been afflicted with. Finally in the teaching of gender and sexuality norms in the Church there is the element "Expected Integration," which serves as a basis for many enforcement tactics discussed in the

"Enforcement" section. Each of these themes will now be further described and illustrated with exemplars.

There's a rule for that role.

To be a man in the Church is a much different experience than to be a woman in the Church. Men are taught to be leaders who can be deacons or monks or priests or bishops or maybe even pope one day. Meanwhile, women are taught to be subservient, with the convent life being the only ordination they can take. As time has passed, many parishes have started allowing both men and women to deliver mass readings, altar serve, and bear gifts. [For my non-Catholic readers: altar servers assist the priest throughout the mass, and gift bearers are the people who bring the bread and wine forward about halfway through the mass for the priest to use for Communion.] However, this is not the case in all parishes, as some will not allow girls to altar serve, as Aubrey found out when her family moved a few states away and she was no longer allowed to altar serve. Aubrey explained:

> I went to the priest, the high priest, the only priest- it's a very small parish. And he looked at me, I had my letters of recommendation from all the priests who adored me as a little kid who was altar serving. And he looked at me and he said, "You are a woman. I will not have women serving in my church. You can be a reader. And that's it." And I was like, I had been the person that everyone called when they needed an altar server, all masses of the week, like whenever they needed somebody that was me. And like, straight up, this guy just took my whole identity. It was like- 'you have a vagina, goodbye.' Like, it was devastating.

Some parishes, as we can see, are more traditional than others when it comes to the proper roles for male and female congregation members. The same is true when diocese are compared to one another. However, one place where the Church has some of its strongest and most conservative influence in the U.S. is in Catholic schools.

The Church's emphasis on gendered rules and roles is evident in everything from school uniforms (Claire noted that Catholic school girl uniforms are supposedly "the perfect presentation of femininity" and that appearance dress codes "were a mile long for girls but had nothing for boys") to being separated to be taught about expectations for them, from purity to shame over normal adolescent behaviors. Claire recalled one instance in eighth grade when she was taken to the lunchroom with all the other girls to be talked to by the deacons. "They told us all the shame about how we need to be good little lambs of God. They did the whole pass-the-chocolate-around. Now the chocolate's dirty—do you want to eat it? No," (Claire). Multiple participants brought up instances of being taught separated by gender to learn about everything from chastity to internet safety, and none of the experiences were positive.

Church teachings around gender are often interwoven with teachings on sexuality, as the Church approaches both from a place of encouraging procreation and traditional roles. Claire explained that through her time as a practicing Catholic, at both school and masses Catholic authorities were "heavily preaching. Gay is bad. One man, one woman, have a baby." Likewise, Indigo also remembers talk of relationships as "always a man and a woman". To paraphrase Emily, the Church is full of well-meaning people who think all rules of gender and sexuality are set in stone.

Queerness as a problem or an affliction.

Every participant described Church teachings on queerness as emphasizing queerness as a bad thing, a problem to be solved, and/or an affliction to be dealt with or overcome. Indigo recounted coming to terms with her bisexuality when she came out to her Catholic friend in high school, only to hear, "Sorry to hear you're struggling with same-sex attraction." Indigo then found herself on the Church's prayer list for what the Church described as her homosexual-attraction struggles.

Other notable codes in this theme were the pattern of telling children that being gay was "dishonorable" (Claire), "against the Bible" (Hannah), or something that outsiders forced upon people, in the case of Sky:

> My mom was like, "Oh, maybe you are gay, or maybe you need help." So that's the roster. So, the mid semester that I met my new friend, my mom found me a therapist with this organization called Catholic Charities. And this White man [was my therapist] and I remember telling him about what I was feeling and what how about what happened with [girl], and the next session he gave me an article about how there's these two girls who are forced to have relationships with each other. Yeah, like he was like, "Sometimes, people make you do things that you don't want to do. You're not that way. But people make you that way." I was like, what the fuck? And I only went to [one more] session because I started realizing that. I think it was low key conversion therapy because he was telling me that like, this wasn't my fault. People do this to you, people force you to do these things like, and he gave me like articles about it. […]. So I stopped seeing him after a while. And I stopped therapy for a bit- for actually a long time because I was scarred after him, because I like this vision of just trying to tell me that I'm wrong, or that what I'm doing is forced upon me or, and it's, that's not the case at all.

Clearly, queerness was regularly referenced as a bad thing in the Church's eyes, and all interviewees noted time(s) they felt they could not talk about queerness in Catholic spaces, since anything outside of the nuclear family was regarded and discussed as bad, wrong, and sinful. In other words, queerness was taught as a problem or an affliction.

Expected integration.

Religious identity often is integrated with personal identity, and Catholicism is no different than other religions in this regard. People born into the Church often refer to themselves as "Cradle Catholics," such as Aubrey and Emily. For these individuals, the integration of Catholicism into everyday life is something that took years to recognize, let alone question. Emily explained:

> I mean, basically, from the day I was born, until I would say, about my first year of college, it was, you know, ingrained that you had to go to church every Sunday. Every Wednesday, you had to attend church. I did extra Bible studies, I participated in TEC (Teens Encounter Christ), all of those things were kind of ingrained as part of the existence of my life, you know, you had to go, there was no questions, you felt sick didn't matter, you had to go.

This description is typical, as to be a good, devout Catholic, one must integrate the religion into every aspect of one's life.

Aubrey, who learned to read at the age of two using Catholic texts, recalled being a small child fixated on this image of Catholicism. "I was really obsessed with the notion of what did it look like to be someone who looked Catholic," she said. Her early childhood was filled with reading Catholic texts and learning about sin and the righteousness of God before the age of seven. Although not every Catholic learns to read at two or has Catholic texts integrated into their early lives as heavily, this notion of sin versus righteousness is taught to children from the time they can understand (and sometimes before).

Emily explained that Church practices were not limited to mass or other Church-sponsored activities, stating, "It's also inside the household. So bringing all of those things, praying before meals, making sure that basically, my life reflected a deacon's daughter kind of persona for a really long time." Even for Catholics not raised by deacons or third order Carmelites, this integration of Catholicism into multifaceted moments and aspects of life was expected to some extent in order to be viewed as a good Catholic.

Enforced

Five themes emerged under gender/sexuality enforcement, which I then broke into two larger categories, "Subtle Enforcement," and "Explicit Enforcement," while leaving the fifth theme, "Who Decides What is Inappropriate?" on its own. Under "Subtle Enforcement" were the themes "Lack of Control" and "Lack of Support." On the other hand, "More Direct Enforcement" included "Punishments" and "Highpoints." Each of these themes will now be further described and illustrated with exemplars.

Subtle enforcement.

The themes that make up subtle enforcement include the lack of control and the lack of support that participants identified in their interviews. Feeling unsupported and like one's life was not in one's own control was described in a variety of ways, as can be seen in the exemplars in the following subsections.

Lack of control.

The first interesting code in this theme was "Coverall to college," coming from the idea of this Catholic Cover-all that Emily explained:

> Catholic or Christian brainwash or cover, the cover-all I think is what they call it, where it's, it's this Christian blanket, and it's been cast over the top of you. So you can't see that

> outside world, you can't see the damage that it's doing, because you're in that safe little space.

In the safe little space in the Catholic coverall, it is easy to not take into consideration anything other than what is said inside that coverall. Blankets do make us feel safe and secure, but as Emily went on to explain, spending one's entire life under one would lead to a lot of people, perspectives, ideas, and experiences getting missed.

Indigo, in particular, mentioned the lack of control she felt when she was in the Catholic school she attended as a child:

> I had previous experience with religions. But going to school somewhere is very different, because it's all encompassing. So even when I would go home, my homework would be religious based. So as a kid, it was a very odd time in my life to not have control over any of that.

This was the most explicit interview quote that came up about lack of control participants felt they had over their bodies, choices, and lives while they were raised Catholic. This lack of control compounded with a lack of support for many participants. Even if we think of children as malleable and complacent, they still have needs for control and support.

Lack of support.

Similar to the above theme, "lack of control," this theme also addresses needs that the participants felt the Church did not meet for them. Lack of support is characterized by not feeling accepted, wanted, and cared for as an individual. First, all participants were raised in households that expected them to succeed and fill all given familial, religious, and task roles, regardless of if their support needs were met.

Aubrey explained this as "coming from a family where praise isn't really given or earned. It's just kind of expected that you're supposed to do well." Many participants echoed these sentiments, stating they, too, had some combination of parents with high expectations and parents who did not give enough support. This resulted in a lot of people pleasing tendencies in my participants, many of whom are still trying to work through these tendencies.

Outside of Catholic households, though, the Catholic Church also does not always offer the kind of support its members need. Claire explained, "Catholic school doesn't offer a lot of assistance when it comes to disabilities and special needs." She expressed that in order to get help with her learning disability, she had to leave Catholic school. Whether this lack of support comes from a lack of resources, a lack of a belief in disability accommodations, or something else entirely remains unclear.

What is clear, at least to Indigo, is that there is a problem with powerful adults in the Church being in positions of control over children. She stated, "Adults in position of power shouldn't have had the emotional access to children having the amount they have." Nuns and priests who teach in Catholic schools spend nearly as much time with kids as their parents do, and when these examples of devout Catholics fail to act in loving, supportive ways, those impressionable children carry the hurt for a long time.

Explicit enforcement.

While it is difficult to look at a person and tell they feel they lack control or support, it is easier to point to behaviors that are used as punishment or rewards. The first theme in this category is therefore "Punishments" and the second is "Positive Reinforcement," which are not rewards *per se* but more or less the highlights of being Catholic.

Punishment.

Catholic schools are notorious for their strict punishments. Even if many will not give children the belt for misbehaving these days, ruler slaps on wrists/hands, being made to stand in the corner holding books above one's head and staying in from recess to write lines from the Bible were all still widely in effect through my participants' upbringings.

Like Claire earlier, Indigo had a learning disability, and was not treated fairly because of it. She explained:

One time when I was in the Catholic school, I couldn't understand what a grading system was. So, I believe I was in first grade, I didn't understand points out of 100. And I asked my teacher because I was failing things because I'm dyslexic. And I didn't understand phonics that was it possible to get an F 100. Like you did so bad that at a certain point it was just good. Like, like a blank slate. So that afternoon, I absolutely bombed a test, and she wrote an F 100 on it and gave it back to me and wrote a note to my parents telling them that I had wanted that grade and asked her about it. And as a first grader, I remember like getting in trouble. Because I wanted to fail when all I had was a genuine question, and that was someone that was supposed to love God and all of His children.

Unfortunately, this was not the only story like this to arise in participant narratives. Many cases of confusion or childhood wonder were turned into examples of what not to do for other children, therefore making the original child feel more guilty than if they were addressed privately or with regard for the child's perspective.

The interviewees listed a variety of punishments that were implemented by either the Catholic Church or its members to encourage conformity. These punishments included exclusions from recesses, being made to write lines of the Bible, getting hands slapped with rulers, and even being made to stand in corners of classrooms holding books over their heads to make them too tired to misbehave. As Emily said, "They put us in boxes we never asked to be put in." This is true for gender and sexuality rules and norms, but it is also true for aspects of people's personalities that were also deemed less than tolerable. By the end of most participants' time practicing Catholicism, they tended to echo Aubrey's statement: "Religion for me was very much like a punishment."

Positive Reinforcement.

However, not everything that happened in the Catholic Church were things that made participants want to leave the religion they were raised in. These highpoints often served as positive reinforcement of the religion. Aubrey loved the church she was raised in, and getting to altar serve would make her week. Claire loved the church choir program because it was where she discovered her love of music. Emily spoke of the great friendships made on Catholic retreats, and Sky got to see some very popular Christian rock bands live at Catholic retreats they attended.

While multiple participants mentioned enjoying seeing their friends at church events, one participant had very positive experiences with the Catholic church and recounted her highlights in their interview. Sky discussed meeting devout Catholic girls through the Church and wanting what they had, which lead her to participate in retreats wholeheartedly and to experiencing Jesus highs. Jesus highs could be ridden for days to months.

All these positive experiences in participants lives as Catholics contributed to their feelings of connectedness to the Church. These positive experiences ranged from simply fun to truly beautiful, and these positive experiences served as examples of good things the Church can provide for its members to entice them to continue to practice Catholicism. This is not to say there is ill intent behind the retreats and other positive sub-organizations of the Church, but instead to point to participants' perceived dichotomy of good things that happened while they were Catholic that made it hard to leave. That is, participants viewed the Church through a positive lens because of their positive associations and experiences until the good experiences could no longer outweigh the negative experiences or the faith was no longer there. But there was one more factor in Church enforcement that lead to confusion, frustration, and resentment in participants, and that factor was concerned with appropriateness.

Who decides what is inappropriate?

Sometimes appropriateness is judged based on expectancy violations, but all participants had their own experiences with the Church, one of its clergy members, or its lay members decreeing something seemingly mundane is in fact inappropriate somehow. In some cases, it is a single clergy member that gets to decide for an entire summer that 13-year-old girls are unable to adequately cover themselves to appropriate modesty standards, as Claire described:

My second incident in the Catholic Church was [when] I decided to volunteer and help the choir teacher [who] had people come in during the summer to lead prayers and lead the songs. And I wanted to because, you know, the choir teacher's really one of my safe people in the school. And music was one of my outlets. So I went. And the church was one of those old churches with no AC and no heating. Everything was broken and falling apart, but it was still thriving. And I had gone wearing a regular short sleeved t shirt and shorts, because it was got awfully hot in the middle of July. And the priest who so happened to be teaching that mass was really, really gross. And the minute he saw me, he went, "Why are you dressed like that?" And I was like, like what? And he's like, "You need to cover up," and I was like, "What do you mean?" He's like, "Your shorts are too short, you're showing too much skin." And I went, "It's hot. Why do I have to cover up? There are other people in the pews who are

> dressed more, more revealing" than what me—a girl at 13—was wearing. So I had to put on a wool like gown in the middle of summer, all because this priest was tempted by a 13-year-old girl. And the girl who was doing the mass with me also had to wear a wool outfit because she had worn shorts too."

She elaborated on how hot and itchy the wool garments were. Through her narrative, it was clear that she felt the priest had turned a non-issue into something inappropriate, which unfortunately led to a summer-long struggle over the issue.

Indigo also described a phenomenon she experienced in her Catholic school that she felt was inappropriate.

> So when I was in kindergarten, they rolled in a TV on September 11. And in real time because I was on the East Coast, I saw the second airplane hit the second tower of the Twin Towers and watched it go down. It's me and a bunch of other five-year-olds and my teacher [and we] held hands and prayed. And that was one of the most traumatic things I've ever seen, because, as anyone who's seen the footage can see, there are literal burning bodies and people jumping out of buildings. But it was more important for us to gather and pray than to shelter the children in that time. I will never forgive the Catholic Church for that.

As Indigo shared, the Catholic school, specifically the nuns running the school, failed to protect the children they oversaw from seeing death and destruction in real time with horrifying detail. In both cases and the others that composed this theme, participants and recipients of these narratives alike were left shaking their heads and asking who decides what is inappropriate. Because of the deferral to Church members' views of what was appropriate in each situation was described by participants as form of control over them, "who decides what's inappropriate?" rounded out the enforcement category.

Tactics for Both Teaching & Enforcement

There were two kinds of tactics that were found to be used for both teaching and enforcing the Church's view on gender, including the way they perceive gender and sexuality to be linked. These tactics were the usage of Tradition and Sacraments, and then a variety of less than loving encounters.

Traditions and Sacraments.

Every participant mentioned at least one Sacrament in their life story narratives. While their associations with these Sacraments ranged from positive to negative with multiple neutrals in the mix, Sacraments, like any cultural ritual, hold power only because we assign them power (Bell 1990; Bell & Kreinath, 2021). Nonetheless, the teachings in preparation for the Sacraments are guides for Catholic life, while encouraging maintenance of a life worthy of the Sacraments serves to enforce Catholic doctrine and ideals.

Of the participants, Aubrey, was by far the most interested in the Sacraments as a child. "Having my first confession- I was so excited to be accountable for my own sins!" she shared, and then laughed. "Makes me kind of sick to think that seven-year-old me was so excited to be more responsible."

As a child every milestone is exciting on its own. But if the Church and/or one's family have taught them that First Confession is to be an exciting rite of passage, it makes sense that someone would be excited to confess sins and hold themselves more accountable. This was especially true in Aubrey's case, as by the time of her first confession as a seven-year-old, she was already fixated on the ideas of sin and righteousness and was being homeschooled with a Catholic curriculum.

The most discussed, and maybe therefore most impactful, Sacrament was Confirmation. Confirmation was much like a graduation for Adam, as not long after he was confirmed he stopped considering himself a practicing Catholic. Meanwhile, Confirmation was a tactic of control for Hannah and Claire both. Hannah did not want to be confirmed, but the private Catholic school she attended would raise her tuition if she was not confirmed, and her parents were unwilling allow her to not be confirmed for that reason. Alice, on the other hand, was pulled back into Catholic school for her eighth-grade year because being enrolled in Catholic school in her city was the easiest way to get confirmed. For Indigo and Juniper both, going to confirmation classes and being confirmed in the Church were ways to spend time with friends and to have guaranteed access to food. Between Aubrey's altar server rejection and the Confirmation sleep away camp, Confirmation marked the end of her faith for Aubrey. On the other hand, because of their experiences at their own sleep away camp for Confirmation, this sacrament marked just the beginning of their spiritual journey for Sky.

While the Catholic Traditions and Sacraments theme had both positive and negative participant experiences that served to teach and enforce Catholic ideals, the next theme that both taught and enforced these ideals was only negative for participants. This negative theme, less than loving encounters, includes everything from exclusion and ignorance to explicit oppression and abuse from Catholics to queer people. This theme of teachings and enforcements is explained further, and with exemplars, next.

Less than loving encounters, from exclusion and ignorance to oppression and abuse.

The largest theme for RQ1, "Less than Loving Encounters" stems from everything from simple comments, such as, "Adam and Eve not Adam and Steve," or "God sends homosexuals to hell" at Sunday masses, to more complex ideas that were rarely explicit. For example, Emily disclosed:

> I grew up saying, what was it, like, "Love thy neighbor as thyself, unless you are an array of things, like a whole list of things." […] And that was like really eye opening to you as seeing all of that because you're like, "You are the one that's telling you to love everybody. But you can't love everybody, unless they fit in this box. So that's your box that you get to live in now."

In other words, it is one thing to say Catholics love everybody and another thing entirely to say that they are loving towards everybody. Emily also recounted her family struggling with even the notion of queerness existing outside of their Catholic bubble:

> My dad has really heavy stances on homosexuality and anything in the queer community, LGBTQIA, he doesn't understand- he doesn't want to understand, realistically, is kind of his stance on it. And because of that, he's very outward with what's the quote, everybody uses, like, "I don't care if you're gay, just don't do it in front of my face," I think is what he likes to tell people, which, obviously, he does not understand the damage that that even just that statement has.

Emily's father, like many other Catholics, wants to sound like he cares about the [queer] people he does not understand, but in so callously writing off a part of a person's identity feels less like love and more like disdain, discrimination, or even hate to the people being discussed with this ignorant attitude. At least some of the Catholic disdain for nonconforming individuals can be chalked up to a willful ignorance. Catholics choosing ignorance on queer populations, queer issues, and other nonconformist ideas they do not partake in can only explain a part of this lack of loving behavior, however.

For example, Aubrey shared her story of coming out to her mother as polyamorous: "I told my mom I was polyamorous and she said, 'at least you're not gay.'" Aubrey, who also identifies as bisexual, laughed before she continued:

> I was like, oh, okay, so I'm like, if- at least I'm not gay. Right. Now. Believe it. At least I don't have a- whatever. My mom- and my mom would probably call me a "try-sexual," [as in] tries everything at least once. I hate- I hate that so much. It's stupid; what a conservative, Republican, asshole thing to say to someone.

Interpersonally speaking, statements that begin with "at least" are not considered supportive statements, and this clearly holds true here in Aubrey's case as well (Barbee et al., 1996; Burleson, 2009). While I was grateful to see that not every participant directly encountered negative messages about queer identities in their immediate families (Adam's parents were accepting and supportive of him from the minute he came out, for example), every participant did share that they heard these messages from Catholics throughout their time in the organization, often in Catholic spaces.

Based on participant narratives, Catholics are not always loving to their own, let alone outsiders. Claire talked extensively of how often she was shamed in Catholic school. At one point she said, "We were basically slut shamed, told that if you're not going to save yourself, for a man and only a man, then you're not worthy of going to heaven." Later in that same lecture she remembered being told that participating in anything sinful, whether it be even as little as kissing someone "meant you will be going to hell," and Claire recounted, "absolutely crying my eyes out in the bathroom because I felt so dirty."

Understandably, participants did not feel loved in these encounters. A common Catholic claim is that to love someone is to want them to go to heaven, but making young people feel these levels of guilt/shame was not perceived as loving by any participants. Even the participants who did find support for their queerness in Catholic spaces told stories of churches and other spaces that were so invested in doing everything as "traditionally" (which means conservatively) as possible.

These themes of teaching, enforcing, and both teaching and enforcing include rules for roles, queerness as a problem or affliction, expected integration, lack of control, lack of support, punishments, highpoints, different definitions of appropriate conduct, Traditions and Sacraments, and less than loving encounters. These tactics, or ways the Church teaches and enforces gender and sexuality norms and traditions, reiterate that actions speak louder than words. Even as Catholics say they love all God's children, their teachings and actions exclude and invalidate for at least some who hear these messages. In the next section I will explore how participants were impacted by these Catholic messages.

Impacts of American Catholic Teachings on Participant Identity Performances

The queer former Catholics that participated in this study shared a variety of impacts being raised Catholic has had on their identity performances. Overarching themes in this section include what it meant to these individuals to be queer and Catholic, the [inherent] burden of queerness, and the four thematic stages of identity shift/understanding.

To Be Queer AND Catholic

First, to be queer and Catholic means a lot of things to a lot of folks, mostly negative. Hannah recalled that being gay in Catholic school was being "by definition, wrong." While children do look up to adults when learning right and wrong, the notion of being wrong comes with the connotation of punishment. As children, some participants would opt to remain silent to avoid even the chance of that punishment, especially when they already felt they were being treated a bit harshly.

For one participant, returning to Catholic school came at the beginning of their own sexual awakening. "Realiz[ing] I'm not straight, but I don't know what I am. And I'm afraid to go back because they're so heavily preaching that Gay is bad." Claire shared:

> You grow up realizing, "Oh, I kind of liked this girl." And then the next day, you go to school, and you're so happy because you're like, "Oh, I really like her." And they're like, "you're going to hell," and I'm like, I'm just gonna stay quiet. It was so stressful. I thought people were gonna look at me and be like, I know what you are."

The fear of discovery was so real for Claire and other participants, especially considering all the ways they found themselves taught and kept within a heteronormative gender binary.

Similarly, Indigo discussed blatant homophobia as a part of life before she had an inkling that she was queer herself:

> I grew up in a time where kids actively played smear the queer, which was a game where you threw the football up in the air and whoever caught it had to run before they got tackled. So like, blatant homophobia was a part of my life.

She continued, "So being queer and Catholic was a very demeaning and debilitating identities to hold."

On the other hand, both Claire and Aubrey share that they hold fond memories for the churches of their youths, despite no longer wanting to be a part of organized religion. Claire was particularly vocal about her Catholic trauma as a queer individual.

> So overall, my experience in the Catholic Church it, it was traumatic, I'm not going to lie, there are a lot of instances that even I don't really talk about, or honestly remember anymore. That hurt me and made me leave a place that I had grown up in and a place that I still do have very fond memories about.

These fond memories may not have been the first memories participants thought of when asked to describe their time practicing Catholicism, but they were apparent in the bittersweet recollections of Aubrey, Alice, and Sky.

However, one participant found strength in this overlap of identities. In college, Sky recognized that it was possible to be queer and Catholic; "It's a possibility that can exist." They recalled being asked regularly, "How are you gay and Catholic?" and responding, "The same way I'm an artist and in theater- I can exist in the two spaces together." Even as some environments make queer folks feel they cannot exist authentically in Catholic spaces; Sky speaks from the other side of the coin. They discussed talking to a gay priest:

> I remember being like, "I, I love being Catholic. I love being gay. And it feels like, I can't fully be in it." And he's like, "I know." He's like, "it is unfortunate that in the Catholic Church, we say that we're accepting," but he's like," we'll accept you being gay, but you can't be too gay". And I was like, "Yeah, that's exactly how I feel."

Some queer people do find spaces of acceptance in the Church, as can be seen in Sky's many queer clergy friends. However, even in more progressive Catholic spaces, they only accept some gayness, some levels of flamboyancy, but not all kinds of queer nonconformity. In other words, even as there are some more accepting spaces for queer people in the Church, there is still a limit to how nonconforming to traditional ideals one can be and still be accepted in those Catholic spaces.

The Burden of Queerness

Drawing on the queer Catholic experience, we must recognize the inherent burden of queerness that exists in our heteronormative society and how much greater that burden is in a religion that does not validate one's queer identity. Indigo explained, "But now I identify as queer. And with that, there comes a burden from even being a child, knowing how people that you thought were good people really thought and felt about you."

This led to a lot of choices for participants. These choices included determining what to identify as and labels to use, but also who to come out to and who to hide themselves from. Adam talked about the time of decision making around his queerness, especially regarding whether or not to come out to Catholic family members:

> I had to make a decision when whether or not to share who I am with people, and I ended up deciding to share it with a select number of people I knew who would accept me for being me and not want to change me.

Meanwhile, Claire discussed coming to realize she had feelings for someone of the same gender while attending Catholic school:

> My best friend in seventh grade ended up being the girl who made me realize I wasn't straight. And like, yeah, did I like boys? Yeah, but right now I really liked my best friend, and my best friend is not a boy.

Developing crushes on friends of the same sex was common among participants, as friends were the first people they got to choose to associate with and were usually the people with whom participants felt most comfortable exploring their most authentic selves. Developing romantic feelings towards a friend is already a burden of developing sexuality, but when those attractions are toward someone of the same gender in a space where that is not typical or accepted, participants experienced a heavy emotional toll. For example, Emily, now a therapist in her community, discussed just how heavy this burden can be on the community:

> I feel like it's not talked about enough. Like, I feel like it's such a very unique [experience]; there's so much religious trauma everywhere. And everyone knows, I mean, if you're Catholic, if you're an LGBTQ, you have religious trauma, or you have childhood trauma. And, it's like, or you have both.

In this quote the level of expected trauma for queer former Catholics is revealed to be rather high.

Being queer comes with an inherent burden, a need to identify oneself and having to label oneself as different. In conservative religious spaces like the Catholic church, this burden of queerness—and the trauma incurred because of the identities one holds—is amplified. Going through these identity constructions and traumatic experiences around holding multiple identities is unique, but there were stages that appeared in the data to show how participants handled these experiences.

Four Thematic Stages of Queer-Religious Identity Reconciliation

In perhaps the most unexpected finding of the present study, I found that every participant spoke to the same four thematic stages when it came to their identity performance and reconciling their Catholic upbringing with their queerness. The four stages exhibited were "Control and Submission," "This Ain't It," "Recovering Catholic," and "Choosing Self." Each stage is described and exemplified in the following sections.

Control and submission.

Participants tended to start their journey with queerness in a "control and submission" stage from being raised Catholic and being taught relationships were to be one man and one woman. All participants expressed some form of submission to the control of Church teachings, be it from family members, a pulpit, or Catholic school. When Emily was discussing how integrated Catholic ideals were into her day-to-day life, she recalled thinking, "Maybe eventually I will believe that stuff too." After all, it was easier to go along with the strict beliefs and stay in favor with one's family and church than to fight against them.

Claire shared, "So many times I would be in such mental anguish that I would be like, I don't believe in God, but I'm still gonna pray." Four other participants shared similar experiences, feeling like one of the only methods of control they had in their Catholic environments was to pray to a deity they no longer believed in.

All participants chose to hide their own identity feelings, chose to only focus on the Catholic teachings they were being fed, or a combination of both. Indigo explained, "If you don't make yourself a target for religious people, they will usually glaze over you and focus on something else." However, making oneself a target often is as simple as living an authentic life for queer folks. Therefore, control and submission were also evident in the hiding of one's identity and other nonconforming beliefs.

"This ain't it."

At some point in each participant's religious journey with the Catholic church, they reached a point where it just no longer made sense for them to continue practicing. This stage was named "this ain't it" because so many participants spoke about this stage callously, and often from a place of frustration and/or desperation for something to change.

For Indigo, this came earlier in her upbringing than it did for others. "After the third grade, I switch to regular public school and had what I would call a pretty tumultuous upbringing in the way that I had been exposed to many religions and had not found God in any of them," she explained. Also, "God never talked to me, and I never understood that they meant figuratively," she continued. By the time she was in eighth grade, despite going through Confirmation in the Church, she was comfortably identifying herself as agnostic.

Emily attempted to avoid reaching this point of contention with her religious identity by convincing herself she had not given the Church enough of a chance. To combat this sense of not belonging, she threw herself into the Church community more than she had before:

> And then in high school, I really tried to get into the church community. I was like, Okay, well, maybe I'm just not giving it a fair shot. So I did Teens Encounter Christ [a kind of retreat weekend]. I did my original weekend. I even did multiple teams [to stay involved]... I did all of those different teams because I thought, "Okay, well, maybe I'm just not reaching in like I should." Like it came back on to me at this point. I was like, "Okay, well, I'm not giving it a go." And through that, you know, I met amazing, great people and became really good friends with them. But I still was like, not agreeing with what I was being taught. I was still like, pushing it to the side and being like, "Okay, well, I'll you know, eventually I'll get there eventually, I'll believe or eventually I'll start to see their- the path that they're on."

Yet, Emily did not come around to believe the same things she was being taught. By the time she got to college and started experiencing life outside of the Catholic bubble, she too had a "this ain't it" moment:

I finally was just like, okay, you know, I gotta look at all these signs that are coming, that are saying, hey, maybe this isn't for you, maybe, maybe it's just not all that it's cracked up to be for some people.

Claire, however, did not realize how much she had moved past her Catholic upbringing until her mother re-enrolled her in Catholic school her eighth-grade year so she could be Confirmed. She explained, "I screamed and cried when I found out she transferred me because I honestly didn't want to go back [to the Catholic school]." By the end of that year of Catholic school, her identity as a member of the LGBTQ+ community was solidified as much as her Catholic faith had crumbled.

For some participants, like Adam, their Catholic faith slowly diminished over time. For others, like Aubrey, a specific moment of losing faith came to mind:

And kind of in that moment, I decided that I didn't believe. I didn't believe that Catholicism was like, all that it was chalked up to be- I didn't have a word for it. But I was like, how can you tell me that God doesn't want me to either serve Him in the way that feels the most meaningful to me? And that some random person who doesn't know me and would like, come at me at this event that I'm literally terrified to be at, knows I'm away from home for the first time, and now decides to make it my problem that my parents are getting a divorce?

Multiple bad experiences with the same clergy were enough to shatter her perceptions of the Church as righteous or the path she was meant to walk. While these participant experiences were varied, feeling like their Catholic upbringing "ain't it" was a core stage in religious-queer identity reconciliation.

"Recovering Catholic": Ideological integration and/or deconstruction.

The third stage of identity reconciliation was originally dubbed "ideological integration and/or deconstruction," until two separate participants used the phrase, "recovering Catholic." There were numerous ways that participants discussed their Catholic upbringing integrating into their lives after leaving the church, both for the positive and the negative.

Participants said that they were glad for their Catholic background giving them a foundation to talk to religious people, particularly Catholics, and also other conservative Christians. Claire said that since leaving the Church, she still regularly uses her Catholic knowledge to handle these interactions, because those people tend not to have defenses when their rhetoric is being used against them. She explained, "Whenever people are like, you're going against God, I'm like, in the book of Judas-, and they're like, how do you know this? I'm like, Catholic school. Don't use the religion against me because I'll use it against you."

Meanwhile, more than half of the participants discussed battling internalized homophobia long after leaving the Church. For example, Indigo said the following:

> I sometimes battle internalized homophobia and think that I am faking it for attention, and I am not actually gay, even though I am in a same sex primary relationship with someone that I would marry. And I still will be like, I don't know if I'm actually gay, as I actively have plans for this person to live with me... seems pretty gay to me. [...] But the internalized homophobia and also not wanting to express myself loudly out of fear for offending other people. And I do think a lot of that has to do with self-preservation.

Indigo's self-preservation was borne from the years in and around conservative religious ideologies, particularly Catholicism.

Another key takeaway from participants' recovering Catholic stage is recognizing that they are not alone in or wrong for feeling the way they do. For example, Hannah shared that she had to come to terms with these feelings. She said, "I am not alone in feeling alienated or wrong or bad for growing up and realizing I was queer, while being a part of a Catholic institution."

As hard as this was for Hannah and other participants, Aubrey and Sky have dealt with ongoing longings to still be Catholic in some way. Aubrey shared that "deconstructing" for her does not mean complete removal from Catholic ideas:

> I'm in a place of religion doesn't make a lot of sense, Catholicism doesn't make a lot of sense. I still believe in saints; I still believe in all of that. I would go to Mass. I miss mass actually pretty regularly. It's a very deep longing in my heart to still be Christian.

She continued, "I think part of my deconstruction is not that I want to leave it behind but is that I wish there was a way to marry the two together, and emotionally I haven't found that place yet."

Similarly, Sky shared, "I do miss it. I miss the community, I miss organization; I miss like, like yearning for bigger and greater things. But I'm good."

Despite these heartfelt longings, participants still continue to deconstruct from—or work to reconstruct their lives without—Catholicism, in order to understand the world through other lenses. While Aubrey expressed the most sadness over no longer being Catholic, she also expressed the most disappointment over the interactions she has had with Catholics since her exit, explaining that when they talk, she has a running train of thought that goes something like, "'Oh, yes, I remember these conversations. They're very naive. Great. Oh, that was close minded. Heard. Oh, I used to believe that. I used to believe that too. I'm sorry.'" She went on to explain her frustrations with those conversations.

> So basically, it's [in] those conversations then I feel patronizing. And that feels extra horrible, right? Because I don't want to be one of those people either. But then I'm being that person inherently by being that person. And I'm just- it's exhausting. I avoid Catholics to save my life.

Avoiding Catholics was another strategy for ideological disintegration that participants cited.

At the end of the day, however, Emily shared maybe the most well-rounded summary of what most participants said of their deconstructions from religion. She shared that this separation has been the greatest challenge of her life so far:

> I think overcoming the ideas of Christianity and how you have to believe a certain thing and act a certain way, look a certain way, you know, behave a certain way. I think that was like a really big challenge for me, because it literally was taking everything I had been taught for so many years, and scratching that and starting fresh, and that's really hard, especially for somebody who is also questioning their sexuality, like, that's a really hard thing to try to do all at once. And it really does, like kind of strip you of everything, you know, and then you're put out into the world trying to figure out where you're at now. And that's really hard.

As Emily shared, it is hard to force oneself to be in a box they do not want to be in, and it is even harder to choose to step out of that box, especially when it is all one has ever known. Being a "Recovering Catholic," was, and probably still is, hard for participants. However, because they were able to take that step out of their box, their Catholic upbringings, they are able to reap the rewards of self-realization and choosing to put themselves before Catholic teachings.

Choosing self, in which identity is more fully realized and embraced.

As hard as it was to re-integrate or deconstruct from Catholic ideologies in participants' lives, every one of them shared that living their more authentic lives now made the struggles of leaving worth it. For example, Claire shared that through therapy, support, self-work, and time to heal, she now knows herself better than before and is happy to be choosing herself.

> What I am, it's not a problem, who I love. It's not a problem. I am not hurting anyone. I am not affecting anyone. And I need to remind myself that almost daily, but it works, and it helps and I'm happy to be in a better place at a better mindset.

Aubrey shared similar growth in her self-esteem, self-worth, and self-confidence. When discussing life philosophies, she explained that she was glad she no longer felt the need to fulfill the subservient, people-pleasing role previously expected of her.

> I believe that my job in life is no longer to make sure everyone else is comfortable in a room. Only my job is to make myself comfortable so that naturally other people who need to be and should be in that space can also be comfortable. (Aubrey).

This shift in perspective for better mental health and self-perception was apparent in all interviews.

Even for the participants whose ideological shifts were not as large or experiences not as tumultuous, altering one's perspective to choosing self and realizing queer identity was perceived as positive, as Adam shared:

> When I shared- began to share that with all the people I wanted to it kind of it was very freeing, in a sense, and it allowed me to be more of who I am. And it felt good, not always, not having to always like purposely hide and change who I am for people.

In other words, choosing to live their most authentic lives meant participants were happier overall. As participants fully realized and embraced their queer identities, they found it was easier to choose themselves and live their lives more authentically. It is important to note that the distinctions between "Recovering Catholic" and "choosing self" are subtle, and some participants embodied both stages at the time of their interviews.

For the participants of this study, religious-queer identity reconciliation ended with choosing their queer identities, or essentially themselves, over their Catholic upbringing. Though they all had varying perspectives on the Church at the time of their interviews, all have chosen to deconstruct from Catholicism and organized religion as a whole at this time. Most of the narratives participants shared about the Church were negative in some aspect, but that is not to say the Catholic Church as a whole is all negative, as will be discussed in the following section.

Exceptions

Through analysis for both research questions, it was made clear that, though there are many negative experiences and associations in regard to the Catholic church and queerness, there are exceptions to many negative Catholic encounters. There are, in fact, Catholic churches that are more progressive and accepting of LGBTQ+ individuals, as Sky shared, even if they are not the majority. There are real allies in the Catholic Church, not only for queer and nonconforming folks, but also for many identities the Church generally does not coexist with, like Pro-Choice Catholics. Many queer people find their place in the Church as Sisters, Brothers, Priests, etc., and go on to be supportive of other queer people through seminary, convents, or other daily practices. Finally, multiple participants quoted the Pope as saying he is not going to stop two men from holding hands in church, nor would he have a problem marrying them. This perspective from the

Pope has outraged many more conservative Catholics since Pope Francis took his office (Gehring, 2016; Puggioni, 2009).

However, this aligns with an unanticipated theme that arose in the interviews with three of the four Latina participants, and that theme was the difference between Hispanic Catholicism and American Catholicism. Not only are Hispanic culture and Catholicism very intertwined, one of my participants went so far as to say, "It was always kind of a given that you would or can be considered Catholic, whether you do actually participate or show up maybe once or twice a year. You're still considered Catholic, you're still baptized, and you go through all the steps."

This was a given for all participants who were raised in Catholic, Hispanic households. Latina participants also described Mexican/Hispanic Catholicism as less harsh and more loving than American Catholicism. This supports the literature that states the USSCB is more conservative and anti-gay than the Church as a whole (Gehring, 2016; Ragojcic, 2016).

Sky themself shared a different perspective on the Church than the other participants. They came from not only a primarily Hispanic Catholic area but also attended private Catholic colleges that were much more liberal than is typical of Catholic institutions in the U.S. for undergrad. This combination allowed for them to foster healthy identity associations with both their Catholicism and their queerness. They explained, "I did feel like being Catholic and being gay really helped me like, be gentle on myself, and like, in my journey, because I felt like the people who were accepting are funny enough people from the church and not my own family." This perspective of love from Catholics for queer people points to both nonconforming individuals' basic interpersonal needs for acceptance and support and also the silver lining that it is possible to be Catholic and actually share the love of Jesus with queer people.

Summary

In this chapter, findings for both research questions were explained. Overall, the Church teaches and enforces its gender and sexuality ideals through a variety of tactics. Participants felt their identity performances were impacted by their Catholic upbringings in a variety of ways, including similar stages of ideological reconciliation. In Chapter V the implications of these findings will be discussed.

CHAPTER V: DISCUSSION

Across this study's body of data, the queer former Catholic participants constructed narratives with similar experiences, as was illustrated by the four thematic stages of ideological and identity constructions and performances, along with the variety of shared experiences regarding Church teachings. Thematic analysis revealed tactics of teaching and enforcement of Catholic gender and sexuality ideals, shared participant experiences of being queer Catholics, carrying the burden of queerness, four stages of ideological reconciliation, and that loving treatment of nonconforming individuals is the exception, not the norm, in American Catholicism. In this chapter, the implications of these findings will be explored.

Summary of Results and Research Considerations

This study had more results than I anticipated when I posed two research questions, but hopefully I can unpack them in a way that makes them more tangible here. To answer RQ1, the Church was perceived to teach gender and sexuality through rules and defined roles, presenting queerness as a problem or affliction, and through expected integration of Catholic ideology into all aspects of daily life. The Church was perceived to enforce gender and sexuality subtly, through removing control and support from participants, and more obviously, through strict punishments and particularly intense highpoints. The enforcement of Catholic gender and sexuality ideals was also evident in the grey area of inappropriateness, as participants found that they often questioned who decided what was or was not inappropriate. Further, the Church both taught and enforced its ideology around gender and sexuality through Tradition and Sacraments, which are integral parts of the Catholic experience, and the less than loving encounters, which ranged from exclusion and ignorance to oppression and abuse.

To answer RQ2, the first findings were the uniqueness of holding the identities queer and Catholic and the inherent burden that comes with being a queer person, and said burden was increased because the of the conflicting identities they held. More unexpectedly, all participants exhibited the same four thematic stages of queer-religious identity reconciliation. These stages were Control and Submission, "This Ain't It," "Recovering Catholic": Ideological Integration and/or Deconstruction, and finally Choosing Self, in which identity is more fully realized and embraced.

At the end of Chapter IV, exceptions to these overarching findings were unpacked. Hispanic Catholicism was perceived by Latina participants to be more loving and less discriminatory than American Catholicism. Further, there were some examples of Catholic individuals and spaces that were more loving, accepting, and supportive than the average ones discussed by participants.

I also would like to address the implications of the "Enforcement" subsection, in which there were far more exemplars from participant narratives of punishment from Catholic entities than there were examples of positive reinforcement. Perhaps this was simply because all participants happened to have chosen to leave the Church and therefore had more negative memories than positive. Perhaps trauma has a part to play, as trauma can cause people to forget all kinds of memories, not just negative ones (Van der Kolk, 1998). However, these two hypothetical explanations likely do not encapsulate the entirety of the implications of this inequality. Instead, this imbalance of good and bad experiences for participants implies that American Catholic entities do not treat queer and nonconforming children, who grow into queer and nonconforming adults, with the love Catholics and other Christians claim to have for everyone. Nonetheless, both punishments and positive reinforcements served to enforce Catholic ideologies around gender and sexuality.

Regarding the four thematic stages of queer-religious identity reconciliation: I chose to call these stages because though they appear linear, they are much like developmental stages which often have overlap as opposed to being defined steps. Recovering Catholic has a different connotation than a lapsed Catholic, because lapsed and non-practicing are synonymous but recovering implies healing and improving after the experiences within American Catholicism. This phrasing also sets participants apart from the normative Catholic idea that once a person is Catholic they always are, even if they are no longer practicing, so instead of being "non-practicing," "lapsed," or otherwise complacent in their inactivity in their religion, while "recovering" also gives more agency to the person or people choosing to distance themselves from the religion in which they were raised.

Contributions to Queer & Religious Identity Literature

This study is a step towards filling in the blanks around the overlap of queerness and religion, particularly American Catholicism. The subsection "Burden of Queernees" not only reflects previous literature describing the unique struggles of queerness (Duxbury, 2014), but also connects this burden of queerness to the additional intersection of [conservative] religious upbringing, such as Catholicism (Etengoff & Daiute, 2015; Gibbs & Goldbach, 2015; Tobin, 2016). Religious literature and queer literature are both extensive, but there is limited literature on the overlap (see Gibbs & Goldbach, 2015; Radojcic, 2016). Findings of this study also support Harris et al. (2008)'s finding that queer people who make religious decisions independent of religious authority have better mental health and fewer internal struggles than their counterparts who defer to religious authority before their own instincts or thoughts.

Literature on church culture is further substantiated by the present study, as there has been a disconnect between various levels of culture and traditional ideological integration. Church culture is old and slow to change, but individual churches can be progressive and supportive (Saroglou et al., 2020; Serini, 2019). The findings of the present study serve as further evidence that churches that adapt more progressive stands on Traditional Catholic and USSCB teachings might be more successful, as the more progressive Catholic Church was successful in Latin America (Mackin, 2010, Serini, 2019).

This study also adds to the body of literature supporting survivors of Catholic and other religious trauma, which will hopefully lead to change that reduces the harm brought into the world through the Church and other religious organizations (Baum, 2011; Fortunato et al., 2021; Gibbs & Goldback, 2015; Radojcic, 2016). This study is particularly like Faulkner and Hecht's (2011) study on being LGBTQ and Jewish and Radojcic's (2016) case study of queer Catholics, and these findings do not contradict with either study's findings. The findings of this study also indicate some of this religious trauma is also an intersectional product of the gender and sexuality norms enforced by the Church, and align with Zuk and Zuk's (2020) aim of drawing attention to and potentially disrupting these Catholic norms—including the interconnectedness of gender identity, gender roles, and sexual orientation—as Catholic power structures that can be detrimental.

Theoretical Implications

First, this study proposes a set of identity reconciliation stages that could become the basis for a larger theory in the future that could be applied to not just religious and queer identities, but a variety of complex identity overlaps. The four stages of queer-religious identity reconciliation mimic previous research. One such mimicry, in terms of stages and identity, is of

Helms' (1993, 1997) model of racial identity development. Both Helms' model and my thematic stages are about coming to terms with having an identity one was previously complacent to or entirely unaware of, but a model of identity development can only reveal part of the picture the present study reveals. Similarly, scholarship on adopting a disabled identity (see Dunn & Burcaw, 2013; Galvin, 2005) aids in conceptualizing the adoption of a new identity—such as disabled or, in the case of this study, queer—and in the trading of one identity for another—such as able-bodied for disabled, or religious for queer, as Aubrey felt she did—but does not help us understand identity overlap or negotiation. However much of the scholarship around disability identity seem to focus on it as a non-identity, which is inherently different from a new identity, such as queer identities discussed in this study. While Paloutzian et al. (1999) posits leaving a religion is not only life-changing but personality-changing as well, this study's thematic stages aligning with the benefits that Gibbs and Goldbach (2015) posit that come from leaving a religion that one does not feel supports them. The second half of the thematic stages found in this study— "Recovering Catholic" and "Choosing Self"—are from participant narratives that were reflective of Austin's (2016) findings of how trans and gender nonconforming folks made sense of their identities, particularly in spaces of oppression.

Also, in the shared space of communication theory and political theory, we see in this study that American Catholicism exhibits the same polarization that exists in all other spheres of American culture, including political and social (Abramowitz & Saunders, 2005). This further connects the Puritanical, conservative roots of America with the exceptionally traditional and rigid American Catholicism (Saroglou et al., 2020; Uhlmann et al., 2011). The USSCB enforcing more traditional views as opposed to Vatican decrees is at least in part responsible for this, but other theories could be utilized to explain this.

Findings of this study reflect or otherwise expand on a variety of scholarship within narrative theory. For example, this study expands Hammack and Cohler's (2009) sensemaking around sexual identity through narrative work by including gender identity and religious identity. Similarly, this work expands upon narrative sense-making by trans and gender nonconforming individuals (Fiani & Han, 2018) by incorporating sexual identity and religious identity.

The present study expands literature for Langellier and Peterson's (2017) narrative performance theory. While the second goal of NPT was less utilized because of its focus on discourse, the first and third goals—the situatedness of narratives in context and the consideration for power structures in the narratives—were notable in the current study. These findings expand NPT beyond family identity work into individual, queer, and religious identity scholarship. Narrative scholarship in general, such as Kraus's (2006) scholarship on identity and belonging, was also expanded upon in part by this study, as participants found that choosing to be their most authentic selves lead to feelings of belonging in spaces that were right for them, such as in their families, friend groups, and community organizations.

Literature on gender as a performance and as a fluid identity or construct (Monro, 2019; Thorne et al., 2019) were also confirmed and expanded with this study. Gibbs and Goldbach's (2015) were echoed twofold in this study; first, parental religious ideas can negatively impact queer children, and second, leaving conservative religious organizations does seem to improve self-perceptions and decrease struggles over identity. Further, as showcased in Table 1, having experienced religious trauma, as all participants self-identified, did make it harder for participants to be religious or spiritual, which aligns with Tobin's (2016) findings.

Practical Implications

Not only are there theoretical implications of the present study's finding, but there are also practical implications. With these findings, hopefully better support can be provided to queer people who were raised in or around the Catholic church. Therapists can benefit from a better understanding of the conflicting experiences that come with being a queer person in the Church, but anyone wishing to better understand or support this minority can also benefit.

Queer former Catholics themselves can benefit from this study in the form of validation and support. Knowing we are not alone with our struggles is such an important part of understanding ourselves, and in deconstructing from conservative religious upbringings. Identity performance is not linear, but support and shared/similar experiences are beneficial for support and healing.

This study also indicates the Catholic Church could better support or otherwise direct other Catholic entities, such as the USSCB. While Latina participants all validated during member checks that they felt Hispanic Catholicism was more loving and/or less harsh than American Catholicism was, at least in their experiences, and participant experiences align with general perceptions of the Latin American pope being more loving and accepting (Gehring, 2016; Puggioni, 2016), more support for the differences in various Catholic cultures is needed to make any concrete claims. However, this points to large-scale divides in universal Roman Catholic Church that aligns with previous research (Maier & Crist, 2017), and the Church could benefit from addressing these divides.

A practical implication of this study also exists for parents. When considering whether to raise a child in a religious organization or to send them to a religious school, consider for a moment if the experiences shared by participants are experiences one would be open to their child having. If not, but a parent still wants to pursue a religious upbringing for their child, they should be aware of these potentialities and be extra diligent in supervising and setting expectations with their children in these settings to keep them safe. Examples of this may include reminding children that they will not be in trouble for telling a parent about something bad that happened to them, or sharing that safe adults do not ask kids to keep secrets from their guardians.

This study also provides further evidence that the Catholic church could benefit from a human resources department for its lay members, not just clergy. In the same vein, this study reveals a possible need for a non-secular authority to oversee places where Catholic children are taught, not to stop religious teachings but to stop any harassment or abuse upon these children.

Study Limitations

One limiting factor of the sample was the sensitive nature of the topic, particularly when considering the safety of the potential participants when asking for their consent and participation. Another limitation of this study was the number of perspectives not able to be captured by eight interviews with a demographic. This is especially true of a demographic as diverse as "queer former Catholics."

This study was conducted with a social constructionist approach. The same study may be entirely different with a different theoretical approach. Comparing the findings of similar studies with different approaches has potential to be enlightening.

Another limitation was the few sources that supported Church doctrine used. While the Catechism was referenced, most other sources that described Catholic doctrine were critical of the Church. While these sources made better connections and arguments that related to the topic at hand, they may not provide the most neutral perspective of the issues discussed or the Church as a whole. There are many groups, organizations, and producers of Catholic literature that support queer Catholics in their journeys, they are just not prominent in the Catholic Church, especially in America. Many queer people who find comfort in Catholicism do pursue lives in convents or parishes as nuns, monks, deacons, and priests, and much of the Catholic literature that is accepting of queerness encourages this path of celibacy.

Directions for Future Research

The number of cases of good intentions leaving lasting harm that came up in these interviews could be their own study. How do good intentions get so turned around? Do the people saying things like "love the sinner, hate the sin," "don't be gay in front of my face," or "at least you aren't gay," really have good intentions with those phrases in the first place? In the cases presented through this study, some clearly are willful ignorance or cop outs, while others are less easy to decipher.

One of the modern expansions of Interpersonal Needs Theory (Schultz, 1958), or INT, which states we have an inherent need for affection, inclusion, and control, could be very useful to study as an explanation for why people leave or feel unsupported by the Church. This study already found queer people who have left the Church feel they had a lack of both control and support while they were practicing Catholics, so incorporating INT would be a logical next step for those findings. Affection and inclusion can both be categorized as support, therefore these findings could potentially expend INT.

Another future study could explore at what point individuals decide the religion they were raised in is not the path they want to continue living on. One of the four thematic stages of religious-queer identity reconciliation found in this study, "This Ain't It," refers to there being a point in which the struggle to maintain the Catholic identity became too great to continue. A study with a larger sample to examine those turning points of religious exits would expand upon this finding substantially.

Personal life philosophies after leaving the Catholic church is another potential future direction from this study. Because participants discussed their struggles with identity performances, it would be enlightening to explore how their religious and spiritual journeys have continued after leaving the church. While not everyone who leaves the Church continues to be religious and/or spiritual, some do, and from these participants, it appears queer people who leave the Catholic church are drawn to paganism. A full study could be conducted to investigate this phenomenon, drawing upon the growing body of literature around the demographic of folks who identify as spiritual but not religious (Ammerman, 2013; Wixwat & Saucier, 2021).

Advice from queer former Catholics to current queer youths and teens in the Catholic church would be another fascinating study to conduct. Participants of this study were not hesitant to share how they would change their upbringings and their encouragements for Catholic kids today. A study of this nature could contribute to both academic literature and support for queer individuals being raised in conservative religions.

Additionally, a correlation study could be done to examine the relationship between the ideological demographics of populations and the polarity of the Catholic churches in those areas. It has been noted that Catholic churches across America vary in how progressive or traditional they are. Because parts of the U.S. are already known to be more conservative or progressive, it would be enlightening to discover if the Catholic ideologies reflect the political alignments of their locations or not.

It would also be fascinating to see how an autoethnography or a variety or ethnographies compared to the stages of identity reconciliation found in this study. If the stages continued to be presented, a theory could then be built from these combined findings. These thematic stages of queer-religious identity reconciliation could be better refined or expanded, as needed.

Finally, an entire other study could be dedicated to the cultural religious overlap of Hispanic and Catholic identities, especially across a broad age range. Multiple generations of Hispanic Catholics were mentioned over the course of the interviews in this theory, and their levels of Catholic ideological saturation seemed to vary extensively. This potential future direction could even include an exploration of Brujaria. I am sure there are more future directions that I do not anticipate at this time, and I am excited to see how this research continues to grow.

Conclusion

Overall, the present study contributes to the body of literature of queer narratives, particularly queer individuals who were raised Catholic. The narratives participants shared offer support for Harris et al. (2008)'s finding that identity decisions made independent of religious doctrine led to lower levels of internalized homophobia and depression, and better self-esteem and mental health. Growing up Catholic and coming to identify as queer was uncomfortable at best and traumatic at worst for participants. Practical implications of this study include better understandings of and support for queer people with Catholic upbringings, especially understanding the stages of identity reconciliation. Personal implications of this study included validation and encouragement. Given that this research stemmed from my personal experiences, it felt good to know I am not alone, even if not all the experiences shared by participants were positive. This study has supported my own development as an academic and individual doing life after overlapping queer and religious trauma, and I hope to continue to support other survivors of these experiences with this work and future work.

www.ingramcontent.com/pod-product-compliance
Lightning Source LLC
LaVergne TN
LVHW010601070526
838199LV00063BA/5029